Gardening
Month by Month
in Manitoba

Laura Peters & Dean Didur

Lone Pine Publishing

The Publisher: Lone Pine Publishing

10145 – 81 Avenue
Edmonton, AB T6E 1W9 Canada
Website: www.lonepinepublishing.com

1808 B Street NW, Suite 140
Auburn, WA, USA 98001

National Library of Canada Cataloguing in Publication Data
Peters, Laura, 1968-
   Gardening month by month in Manitoba / Laura Peters & Dean Didur.

   ISBN 1-55105-400-0

   1. Gardening--Manitoba--Calendars. I. Didur, Dean, 1956- II. Title.
SB453.3.C2P485 2003   635'.097127   C2003-910934-8

Editorial Director: Nancy Foulds
Project Editor: Sandra Bit
Research Assistant: Don Williamson
Production Manager: Gene Longson
Design & Layout: Heather Markham

Maps & Climate Charts: Jeff Fedorkiw, Elliot Engley
Cover Design: Gerry Dotto
Principal Photographers: Tamara Eder, Tim Matheson
Illustrations: Ian Sheldon
Scanning, Separations & Film: Elite Lithographers Co.

Front cover photographs (clockwise from top right): by Tamara Eder, false sunflower, poppy, sweet potato vine, climbing rose 'Lichtkonigen Lucia', hybrid tea rose 'Just Joey'; *by Tim Matheson,* dahlia, daylily, cushion spurge.

The photographs in this book are reproduced with the generous permission of their copyright holders.

All other photos: All-American Selections 75a, 99c, 120–121, 127b; Joan de Grey 137d; Therese D'Monte 70; Dean Didur 17a, 21d, 147a, 147b; Don Doucette 15a, 21a, 23b; Elliot Engley 31a, 31c, 33a, 33b; EuroAmerican 19a; Jennifer Fafard 123b, 123c, 125b, 125c, 127a, 129c, 131a, 131b, 132–133, 151a, 151b, 151c, 155c; Anne Gordon 137c; Saxon Holt 35b; Trevor Horbachewsky 129b; Horticolor©Nova-Photographik/Horticolor 94; Linda Kershaw 39c; Colin Laroque 96–97; Dawn Loewen 143b; Janet Loughrey 137b; Heather Markham 35d, 57b, 79c, 117b, 143d; Marilyn McAra 43b, 115a, 115b, 115d; Kim O'Leary 29b, 35a, 87b, 111a; Alison Penko 27a, 113c; Laura Peters 81b, 81d, 119c; Robert Ritchie 59a, 86; Peter Thompstone 51c, 105a, 141a; Don Williamson 15b, 119a, 135b, 144–145, 148.

Frost date and hardiness zone maps: information taken from *The Atlas of Canada* (http://atlas.gc.ca) ©2002. Her Majesty the Queen in Right of Canada with permission of Natural Resources Canada. *Climate normals and extremes charts:* adapted from the Meteorological Service of Canada, with permission from Environment Canada.

We acknowledge the financial support of the Government of Canada through the Book Publishing Industry Development Program (BPIDP) for our publishing activities.

PC: 08

INTRODUCTION

Manitoba, the 'Keystone Province,' is located near the geographical centre of North America. The northern part of the province is made up of rugged terrain and remote, vast pine forests, lakes and rivers. Prime agricultural land lies in a triangle bordering Saskatchewan and the U.S., and cutting diagonally across Lake Winnipeg. Manitoba is a fairly level province with some slopes interspersed among rolling hills over 820 m (2706') high. Manitoba's 650 087 km^2 (250 934 mi^2) of land surface includes over 101 592 km^2 (39 215 mi^2) of inland water. The bulk of the province's population resides throughout the central and southern regions, and over half lives in Winnipeg.

Unique to Manitoba is the mighty Red River, which flows north from North Dakota. All waters in Manitoba flow to Hudson Bay. Before the province was settled, a large area of south and central Manitoba was flood plain or swamp. Though an extensive system of drainage ditches was constructed throughout this region, devastating floods are always a possibility. In the past, The Red River has been known to become the "Red Sea," displacing tens of thousands of people.

Most of Manitoba is formed on an ancient seabed. Eons of flooding, draining and accumulated silt have left us with some of the best topsoil in the world. Some deposits of sandy soil exist in various areas throughout the central and southern regions, and, in many areas, a layer of dense clay lies just beneath the topsoil. Though some soils are acidic, in general, the soil tends to be neutral to alkaline.

Manitoba's climate, characterized by warm, sunny summers and cold, bright winters, is not without its challenges, and some research and experimentation are required to get the best results from your garden. The growing season can be short, about 110 frost-free days. But the long hours of daylight more than make up for the short season, providing plants with plenty of growing hours over the summer. Similar to other prairie provinces, Manitoba experiences an average of 2200 hours of sunshine annually. Although the province has a similar range of

a backyard prairie garden

hardiness zones as Alberta and Saskatchewan, 0a–3a, the percentage of humidity tends to be slightly higher. Many plants actually prefer the cool nights and low to moderate humidity that are common here.

Precipitation is possibly the most variable climatic factor influencing our gardens. More than half of the annual precipitation occurs during the summer, often in short, heavy showers. Annual snowfall averages 110–140 cm (44–56"). Though rain can be regular and adequate during the growing season, it is just as possible to experience

gazanias

bridge pathway (*above*); mini alpine garden (*below*)

naturalistic water feature (*below*)

drought conditions or excessive rain. As with all the factors that influence our gardens, we must be prepared to make the most of what nature offers us and try to take up the slack where it lets off.

What grows naturally in an area can indicate what will also grow well in our gardens. The truer indication of the bounty gardeners here have to choose from, however, is the variety of plant material and garden designs displayed in Manitoba gardens, which reflect the style and enthusiasm of those determined gardeners willing to try anything just to see how it will grow. Many plants that are classified "out of zone" do very well here in the right location, and every imaginable style of garden can be created, from wildflower drifts to shaded woodland pathways to formal knot gardens.

Where we garden varies almost as much as what we garden. Apartment and condo dwellers enjoy container gardening; rural gardeners may be tilling the same soil their great-grandparents did; urban gardeners may live in older neighbourhoods where the topsoil is deep, or they may struggle with the thin layer of soil common to new subdivisions. Beautiful, successful gardens are possible in all these situations, limited only by the imagination of the gardener.

This book should give you ideas and help you plan what to do in your garden and when. Some tasks are listed in the months you would most likely do them while others can be done at various times through the year. There is also space for you to write in your own thoughts and ideas.

The information in this book is general. If you need to find more detailed information on a topic,

English wallflower with lobelia and aubrieta (rockcress)

refer to the back of the book where we have listed some resources for you. Gardening courses are offered through colleges, continuing education programs, gardening clubs and through Master Gardener programs. You can tackle even the most daunting gardening task once you are prepared and well informed.

Use the book to keep track of unusual weather conditions, when plants sprout and when they first flower. Note any unusual insects or

golden marguerites

birds you see in your garden. If a plant was problematic in a certain location, you will remember that next year if you write it in your book. Jot down your inspirations for future garden design plans or any successes you've had with this year's plantings. You'll appreciate it next spring when memories of last year's garden are getting a little fuzzy.

delphinium with rudbeckia (black-eyed Susan)

hot peppers

There are no absolute rules when it comes to gardening. As prairie gardeners, we must take advantage of everything each season has to offer. Extraordinary opportunities are available to gardeners of every level of expertise, especially those north of the 49th parallel. No two years are identical, and all information should be taken with a pinch of salt. Use your own best judgement when deciding when to do things in your garden. Above all else, always take time to enjoy your Manitoba garden.

MANITOBA CLIMATE NORMALS 1971–2000

(Adapted from the Meteorological Service of Canada data
as posted on the Environment Canada website)

	CATEGORY	JAN	FEB	MAR	APR	MAY	JUN	JUL	AUG	SEP	OCT	NOV	DEC	YEAR
ASHERN	DAILY MAXIMUM (°C)	-13.3	-9.4	-1.6	9.6	18.1	22.5	25.3	23.8	17.0	9.8	-1.6	-11.2	7.4
	DAILY MINIMUM (°C)	-25.2	-22.1	-13.9	-3.6	4.0	8.8	11.5	10.0	4.6	-0.8	-10.4	-21.7	-4.9
	RAINFALL (MM)	0.2	0.0	6.2	17.9	46.9	87.4	61.1	80.7	59.8	30.9	3.7	1.2	395.9
	SNOWFALL (CM)	16.9	12.8	17.4	11.0	3.3	0.0	0.0	0.0	1.1	7.2	18.1	16.4	104.0
	*PRECIPITATION (MM)	17.1	12.8	23.5	28.9	50.2	87.4	61.1	80.7	60.8	38.2	21.7	17.5	499.9
BRANDON	DAILY MAXIMUM (°C)	-12.6	-8.2	-1.1	9.8	18.6	22.8	25.2	24.8	18.3	10.8	-1.1	-9.7	8.1
	DAILY MINIMUM (°C)	-23.5	-19.3	-11.8	-2.9	4.1	9.3	11.4	10.1	4.4	-2.1	-11.1	-20.0	-4.3
	RAINFALL (MM)	0.2	0.7	5.1	20.1	50.1	74.4	75.8	69.2	49.9	22.2	4.2	1.2	373.1
	SNOWFALL (CM)	22.1	15.6	18.1	10.7	2.7	0.0	0.0	0.0	0.3	5.8	15.9	21.0	112.0
	PRECIPITATION (MM)	18.0	14.1	22.2	31.0	52.7	74.4	75.8	69.2	50.1	27.7	17.7	19.2	472.0
CHURCHIL	DAILY MAXIMUM (°C)	-22.7	-20.4	-14.5	-5.0	3.2	11.4	17.3	16.3	8.8	1.1	-8.9	-18.8	-2.7
	DAILY MINIMUM (°C)	-30.7	-28.9	-24.4	-14.5	-4.6	1.7	6.8	7.2	2.5	-4.5	-16.1	-26.8	-11.0
	RAINFALL (MM)	0.0	0.1	0.3	1.3	17.8	40.8	56.0	68.3	57.5	20.9	1.2	0.2	264.4
	SNOWFALL (CM)	19.8	18.3	18.3	19.8	15.4	3.4	0.0	0.0	6.0	28.7	37.0	24.2	191.0
	PRECIPITATION (MM)	16.9	15.7	16.1	19.0	31.9	44.3	56.0	68.3	63.4	46.9	33.1	20.0	431.6
DAUPHIN	DAILY MAXIMUM (°C)	-11.9	-7.8	-0.9	9.5	18.2	22.4	24.9	24.2	17.5	10.4	-0.9	-9.3	8.0
	DAILY MINIMUM (°C)	-22.6	-18.9	-12.0	-3.3	3.7	9.1	11.9	10.4	5.0	-1.1	-10.2	-19.5	-4.0
	RAINFALL (MM)	0.3	0.2	4.4	15.1	51.1	86.9	75.9	60.4	66.1	30.2	3.4	0.7	394.6
	SNOWFALL (CM)	20.1	16.5	22.9	13.6	4.2	0.2	0.0	0.0	1.6	6.0	20.7	23.0	128.7
	PRECIPITATION (MM)	17.5	13.2	25.3	28.2	54.3	87.1	75.9	60.4	67.6	36.1	22.1	20.1	507.7
FLIN FLON	DAILY MAXIMUM (°C)	-16.6	-11.0	-2.9	6.9	15.0	20.4	23.1	21.8	14.2	6.2	-5.1	-14.0	4.8
	DAILY MINIMUM (°C)	-26.2	-22.3	-15.8	-5.5	2.6	9.3	12.6	11.4	5.4	-0.8	-11.7	-22.6	-5.3
	RAINFALL (MM)	0.1	0.3	0.9	8.6	36.9	66.6	76.5	66.6	55.3	25.6	1.4	0.4	339.2
	SNOWFALL (CM)	19.6	14.6	19.1	20.0	3.7	0.0	0.0	0.0	2.0	13.0	25.4	23.9	141.3
	PRECIPITATION (MM)	17.6	13.4	19.0	28.3	40.6	66.6	76.5	66.6	57.3	38.3	24.8	21.8	470.8
GIMLI	DAILY MAXIMUM (°C)	-12.8	-9.3	-1.8	8.2	16.3	21.6	24.9	23.2	16.9	9.5	-1.1	-10.5	7.1
	DAILY MINIMUM (°C)	-23.5	-20.3	-12.8	-2.9	4.7	10.5	13.5	11.8	6.3	0.0	-9.2	-20.3	-3.5
	RAINFALL (MM)	0.3	0.3	8.8	19.8	47.6	94.1	69.7	64.2	65.6	30.3	5.3	1.8	407.8
	SNOWFALL (CM)	27.6	21.7	24.1	11.4	2.2	0.0	0.0	0.0	1.1	8.4	26.6	25.0	148.1
	PRECIPITATION (MM)	22.2	17.3	30.0	30.0	49.8	94.1	69.7	64.2	66.7	38.3	27.6	22.5	532.5

* equivalent to rainfall

MANITOBA CLIMATE NORMALS 1971–2000
(Adapted from the Meteorological Service of Canada data as posted on the Environment Canada website)

CATEGORY	JAN	FEB	MAR	APR	MAY	JUN	JUL	AUG	SEP	OCT	NOV	DEC	YEAR
DAILY MAXIMUM (°C)	-11.0	-7.2	-0.6	10.4	19.4	23.6	25.9	25.3	19.1	11.2	-0.5	-8.3	8.9
DAILY MINIMUM (°C)	-20.1	-16.2	-9.2	-1.0	6.2	11.8	14.2	12.9	7.6	1.3	-8.0	-16.6	-1.4
RAINFALL (MM)	0.4	1.6	6.4	24.5	61.6	84.4	71.2	69.9	52.5	37.8	3.7	2.3	416.2
SNOWFALL (CM)	19.5	17.6	20.0	11.1	1.7	0.0	0.0	0.0	0.3	7.0	24.0	18.5	119.7
PRECIPITATION (MM)	19.2	19.2	25.0	35.5	63.3	84.4	71.2	69.9	52.7	44.8	27.4	20.8	533.3
DAILY MAXIMUM (°C)	-12.0	-8.4	-1.3	9.6	18.8	23.2	25.4	24.6	18.2	10.8	-0.6	-9.2	8.3
DAILY MINIMUM (°C)	-22.6	-19.4	-11.6	-2.4	5.0	10.9	13.2	11.5	5.9	-0.1	-9.1	-18.9	-3.2
RAINFALL (MM)	0.2	0.1	6.9	22.3	45.9	75.8	75.2	70.3	53.5	31.0	5.2	2.7	389.1
SNOWFALL (CM)	23.6	17.7	20.2	9.6	1.9	0.0	0.0	0.0	0.4	7.2	21.2	23.7	125.5
PRECIPITATION (MM)	23.8	17.8	27.0	31.9	47.8	75.8	75.2	70.3	53.9	38.2	26.5	26.3	514.5
DAILY MAXIMUM (°C)	-11.4	-7.0	0.1	10.1	18.8	23.0	25.3	24.4	18.1	10.7	-0.9	-8.7	8.5
DAILY MINIMUM (°C)	-23.4	-19.5	11.8	-3.0	4.1	9.5	12.0	10.5	5.3	-0.5	-9.6	-19.2	-3.8
RAINFALL (MM)	0.0	2.6	9.0	26.7	62.3	95.6	94.1	78.2	70.1	38.1	9.6	0.7	487.1
SNOWFALL (CM)	26.1	19.3	17.0	7.3	0.6	0.0	0.0	0.0	0.2	4.5	24.4	23.7	123.0
PRECIPITATION (MM)	26.2	21.8	26.0	34.0	63.0	95.6	94.1	78.2	70.3	42.6	34.0	24.4	610.1
DAILY MAXIMUM (°C)	-15.8	-10.6	-2.9	7.0	15.4	20.7	23.4	22.2	14.9	7.2	-4.1	-13.0	5.4
DAILY MINIMUM (°C)	-25.5	-21.6	-14.9	-5.0	2.6	8.9	12.0	10.8	5.0	-1.0	-11.4	-21.9	-5.2
RAINFALL (MM)	0.1	0.4	2.1	10.0	32.2	67.6	64.8	62.5	54.2	27.3	2.4	0.3	323.8
SNOWFALL (CM)	23.0	18.6	22.5	18.1	4.3	0.0	0.0	0.0	1.4	14.6	26.9	25.6	154.9
PRECIPITATION (MM)	16.1	13.4	19.2	25.9	36.3	67.6	64.8	62.5	55.4	40.3	23.0	18.3	442.8
DAILY MAXIMUM (°C)	-19.4	-13.7	-5.2	4.9	13.4	19.7	22.7	21.0	12.8	4.3	-7.3	-16.7	3.0
DAILY MINIMUM (°C)	-30.5	-27.0	-20.5	-9.2	-0.4	5.5	8.9	7.2	1.5	-4.3	-16.6	-27.2	-9.4
RAINFALL (MM)	0.1	0.2	0.8	6.2	33.0	67.9	86.1	73.7	58.5	19.9	1.6	0.2	348.2
SNOWFALL (CM)	21.1	18.0	21.6	20.8	12.0	1.4	0.0	0.1	3.9	22.1	35.0	30.2	186.2
PRECIPITATION (MM)	18.2	15.9	20.6	26.0	44.4	69.4	86.1	73.9	62.4	41.4	32.8	26.3	517.4
DAILY MAXIMUM (°C)	-12.7	-8.5	-1.1	10.3	19.2	23.3	25.8	25.0	18.6	10.8	-0.9	-9.7	8.3
DAILY MINIMUM (°C)	-22.8	-18.7	-11.0	-2.4	4.8	10.7	13.3	11.9	6.0	-0.3	-9.6	-19.1	-3.1
RAINFALL (MM)	0.2	2.5	7.5	21.5	58.0	89.5	70.6	75.1	51.9	31.0	6.1	1.6	415.6
SNOWFALL (CM)	23.1	14.2	15.8	10.1	0.8	0.0	0.0	0.0	0.4	5.0	21.4	19.8	110.6
PRECIPITATION (MM)	19.7	14.9	21.5	31.9	58.8	89.5	70.6	75.1	52.3	36.0	25.0	18.5	513.7

MORDEN

PORTAGE LA PRAIRIE

SPRAGUE

THE PAS

THOMPSON

WINNIPEG

MANITOBA CLIMATE EXTREMES 1971–2000
(Adapted from the Meteorological Service of Canada data
as posted on the Environment Canada website)

ASHERN

MAXIMUM (°C)	37.5 ON AUGUST 6, 1988
MINIMUM (°C)	-47.2 ON JANUARY 6, 1968
DAILY RAINFALL (MM)	137.6 ON AUGUST 20, 1980
DAILY SNOWFALL (CM)	31.0 ON APRIL 27, 1966
SNOW DEPTH (CM)	89.0 ON MARCH 24, 1964

MORDEN

MAXIMUM (°C)	43.9 ON JULY 11, 1936
MINIMUM (°C)	-42.0 ON JANUARY 16, 199
DAILY RAINFALL (MM)	150.0 ON AUGUST 17, 199!
DAILY SNOWFALL (CM)	53.3 ON APRIL 5, 1997
SNOW DEPTH (CM)	79.0 ON FEBRUARY 28, 19;

BRANDON

MAXIMUM (°C)	38.5 ON AUGUST 6, 1988
MINIMUM (°C)	-45.6 ON JANUARY 7, 1966
DAILY RAINFALL (MM)	86.4 ON MAY 6, 1964
DAILY SNOWFALL (CM)	34.3 ON OCTOBER 10, 1959
SNOW DEPTH (CM)	89.0 ON FEBRUARY 28, 1969

PORTAGE LA PRAIRIE

MAXIMUM (°C)	39.5 ON AUGUST 4, 1983
MINIMUM (°C)	-44.0 ON FEBRUARY 2, 199
DAILY RAINFALL (MM)	96.0 ON AUGUST 14, 1987
DAILY SNOWFALL (CM)	49.0 ON APRIL 27, 1966
SNOW DEPTH (CM)	109.0 ON MARCH 31, 1965

CHURCHILL

MAXIMUM (°C)	36.9 ON AUGUST 11, 1991
MINIMUM (°C)	-45.4 ON FEBRUARY 13, 1979
DAILY RAINFALL (MM)	62.3 ON SEPTEMBER 3, 1983
DAILY SNOWFALL (CM)	47.6 ON MAY 17, 1978
SNOW DEPTH (CM)	148.0 ON APRIL 21, 1955

SPRAGUE

MAXIMUM (°C)	38.9 ON JULY 12, 1936
MINIMUM (°C)	-48.3 ON JANUARY 30, 195
DAILY RAINFALL (MM)	109.0 ON AUGUST 3, 1985
DAILY SNOWFALL (CM)	33.0 ON OCTOBER 18, 191;
SNOW DEPTH (CM)	113.0 ON FEBRUARY 28, 19

DAUPHIN

MAXIMUM (°C)	39.2 ON MAY 22, 1980
MINIMUM (°C)	-44.4 ON FEBRUARY 18, 1966
DAILY RAINFALL (MM)	100.3 ON JUNE 18, 1956
DAILY SNOWFALL (CM)	26.2 ON NOVEMBER 13, 1973
SNOW DEPTH (CM)	102.0 ON FEBRUARY 14, 1956

THE PAS

MAXIMUM (°C)	36.7 ON JULY 20, 1955
MINIMUM (°C)	-49.4 ON FEBRUARY 18, 19
DAILY RAINFALL (MM)	93.0 ON JULY 11, 1994
DAILY SNOWFALL (CM)	37.3 ON MARCH 21, 1962
SNOW DEPTH (CM)	144.0 ON MARCH 9, 1956

FLIN FLON

MAXIMUM (°C)	35.0 ON JUNE 5, 1988
MINIMUM (°C)	-45.6 ON FEBRUARY 1, 1974
DAILY RAINFALL (MM)	78.2 ON JULY 23, 1981
DAILY SNOWFALL (CM)	39.4 ON APRIL 20, 1973
SNOW DEPTH (CM)	67.0 ON FEBRUARY 18, 1992

THOMPSON

MAXIMUM (°C)	37.4 ON JUNE 18, 1995
MINIMUM (°C)	-48.9 ON JANUARY 8, 1968
DAILY RAINFALL (MM)	75.3 ON AUGUST 25, 1997
DAILY SNOWFALL (CM)	45.7 ON OCTOBER 6, 1970
SNOW DEPTH (CM)	91.0 ON JANUARY 29, 1968

GIMLI

MAXIMUM (°C)	37.5 ON AUGUST 4, 1983
MINIMUM (°C)	-41.2 ON JANUARY 20, 1982
DAILY RAINFALL (MM)	104.8 ON JUNE 12, 1989
DAILY SNOWFALL (CM)	31.4 ON NOVEMBER 8, 1986
SNOW DEPTH (CM)	57.0 ON APRIL 5, 1979

WINNIPEG

MAXIMUM (°C)	40.6 ON AUGUST 7, 1949
MINIMUM (°C)	-45.0 ON FEBRUARY 18, 19
DAILY RAINFALL (MM)	83.8 ON AUGUST 11, 1962
DAILY SNOWFALL (CM)	35.6 ON MARCH 4, 1966
SNOW DEPTH (CM)	91.0 ON JANUARY 30, 1956

FROST DATE MAPS

HARDINESS ZONE MAP

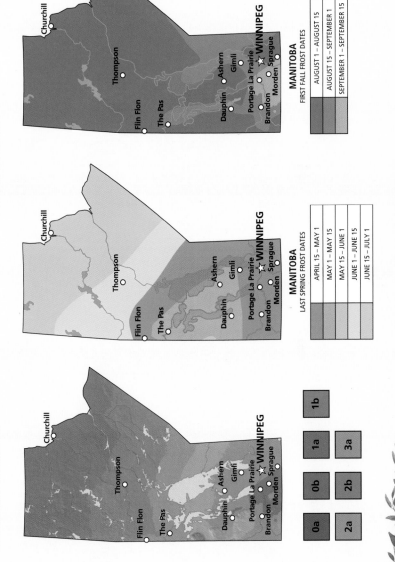

MANITOBA
FIRST FALL FROST DATES

	AUGUST 1 – AUGUST 15
	AUGUST 15 – SEPTEMBER 1
	SEPTEMBER 1 – SEPTEMBER 15

MANITOBA
LAST SPRING FROST DATES

	APRIL 15 – MAY 1
	MAY 1 – MAY 15
	MAY 15 – JUNE 1
	JUNE 1 – JUNE 15
	JUNE 15 – JULY 1

0a	0b	1a	1b
2a	2b	3a	

Churchill
Thompson
Flin Flon
The Pas
Dauphin
Ashern
Gimli
Portage La Prairie
Brandon
Morden
Sprague
WINNIPEG

JANUARY

Now is the time to reflect and dream of warm sunny days and grand garden designs.

JANUARY

1

2

Avoid using chemical de-icers because they are harmful to lawns and garden plants.

3

4

If you had a real Christmas tree, an alternative to recycling is to cut it up and use the branches as a mulch to shelter low-growing shrubs and groundcovers.

5

6

7

One of the flowers you might dream of adding to your garden is the shrub rose 'Martin Frobisher' (*left*). Hardy to zone 2, this vigorous rose produces sweetly scented double pink flowers from early summer to fall. Cotoneaster hedge in winter (*right*)

Don't forget to top up your bird-feeders regularly. Feeding the birds encourages them to keep visiting in summer when they will help keep your insect pest populations under control.

Typically, January offers a reliable blanket of snow throughout the prairies. However, in some years, snow is in short supply or completely absent from the landscape, exposing the bare ground and unprotected plants to our often bitter northern winters. When there is little insulating snow, or when it melts too quickly or too early, plants are left vulnerable to the stressful cycles of freezing and thawing. A good, thick fall mulch can prove to be worth its weight in gold in a snowless year or in a snowless area.

THINGS TO DO

January is one of the hardest months for the garden and the easiest for the gardener.

Snow is the garden's best friend. Pile clean snow on snowless garden beds to insulate them against the wind and cold. Some people refer to this as "snow farming."

JANUARY

8

9

Avoid placing houseplants in hot or cold drafts.

10

11

Order gardening and seed catalogues to look through even if you don't start your own seeds.

12

13

14

Begonias (*left*) can be brought indoors in fall and kept as houseplants in a sunny location through the winter. Ornamental grass (*right*)

Gently brush snow off the branches of evergreens such as cedars, but leave any ice that forms to melt naturally. The weight of the snow or ice can permanently bend flexible branches, but more damage is done trying to remove ice than is done through its weight.

Choose and order seeds for early starting. Sort through the seeds you have, test them for viability and throw out any that don't germinate or that you won't grow. Trade seeds with gardening friends.

Get lawn mowers and other power tools serviced now. They will be ready for use in spring, and you may get a better price before the spring rush.

Annual poppy seeds are easy to collect and share. Both Iceland poppies (*right*) and peony-flowered poppies (*top right*) are available in a variety of colours.

To test older seeds for viability, place 10 seeds between two layers of moist paper towel and put them in a sealed container. Keep the paper evenly dampened but not too wet. Seeds may rot if the paper towel is too moist. Check each day to see if the seeds have sprouted. If less than half the seeds sprout, buy new ones.

15

16

17

18

19

20

Reduce watering of houseplants because most need little water during winter.

The datura (*left*) is an elegant, exotic-looking plant that produces large, showy, scented flowers. Daturas are relatively new to the prairie garden scene. Coleus (*top right*); English ivy topiary (*bottom right*)

Clean the foliage of your house-plants. When light levels are low, it is important for plants to be able to use whatever light is available. As a bonus, you might help reduce insect populations because their eggs will be wiped off along with the dust.

Check houseplants regularly for common indoor insect pests such as whiteflies, spider mites and mealybugs.

GARDEN DESIGN

What would it take to improve winter interest in your yard? Now is the time to determine what is missing in your winter vista. Persistent fruit, unusual bark and branch patterns, evergreens and colourfully stemmed shrubs can enliven a stark winter landscape.

Most indoor plants will benefit from increased humidity levels. Place pots on a tray of pebbles. If you add water to the pebbles when needed, you will increase the humidity through evaporation but prevent water-logged roots.

JANUARY

21

22

January is a great time for garden planning. In winter, the bones of the garden are laid bare, so you can take a good look at the garden's overall structure.

23

24

25

26

27

Rosehips (*left*); the red stems of red-twig dogwood and the bright berries of viburnum (*top right*); the seedpods of amur maple (*centre right*); and the peeling bark of birch (*bottom right*) add interest to the garden in winter.

Plants that add variety to a winter garden

- Amur Cherry (*Prunus maackii*): coppery, peeling bark
- Amur Maple (*Acer ginnala*): attractive bark; branching pattern
- Cedar (*Thuja* spp.) or Juniper (*Juniperus* spp.): evergreen branches
- Clematis (*Clematis* spp.): fuzzy seedheads
- Dogwoods (*Cornus* spp.): red, purple or yellow stems
- Highbush Cranberry (*Viburnum trilobum*): bright red berries
- Mountain Ash (*Sorbus* spp.): persistent red berries
- Paper Birch (*Betula papyrifera*): attractive white bark, peels in layers
- Shrub Roses (*Rosa* spp.): brightly coloured hips
- Winged Burning Bush (*Euonymus alatus*): corky ridges on the branches

JANUARY

28

29

*Imagine the garden you'd like to have,
and keep this notebook and your diagrams
at hand so you can jot down ideas
as they come to you.*

30

31

Woody evergreens, such
as cedar (*left*), upright
juniper (*top right*) and
white spruce (*far right*),
add interesting texture
and rich green colour to
a sometimes monotonous
winter landscape.

PROBLEM AREAS IN THE GARDEN

Keep track of these potential problem areas in your garden:

- windswept areas: perhaps a tree, shrub or hedge could be added next summer to provide shelter

- snowfree areas: places where the snow is always quick to melt are poor choices for very tender plants, which benefit most from the protection of the snow

- snowbound areas: places where the snow is slowest to melt provide the most protection to plants but stay frozen longest in spring, making them poor locations for spring-flowering plants.

Spruce are widely grown in our province, and new varieties are available almost every gardening season. They are well suited to our harsh winters, and some, like the Colorado blue spruce (*left*), provide a rich blue-green colour contrast against white snow.

FEBRUARY

*Cycles of warm and cold begin to
weave through the longer days as we
await signs of spring.*

FEBRUARY

1

2

*Finish ordering plants and seeds
from catalogues.*

3

4

*Pile extra snow over perennials and shrubs
if snow cover is sparse.*

5

6

7

Colourful little crabapples often remain on the
branches of the tree through winter, a reminder of
the beautiful blossoms to come in spring
(*left*). Flowering crabapple trees in
spring (*bottom right*)

Groundhog Day, though a novelty, has little bearing on our wish for an early spring since, shadow or no shadow, we will likely experience at least six more weeks of winter. Despite the continuing cold, gardeners are not without things to do. Seeding indoors can significantly extend our growing season, and February is the month to get started.

THINGS TO DO

February is another month with few tasks, but preparations can be made now that will keep things moving smoothly once the season kicks into high gear.

Check shrubs and trees for storm-damaged branches, and remove them using proper pruning techniques.

Cut branches of flowering shrubs, such as forsythia (*above*), crabapple and cherry, to bring indoors. Placed in a bright location in a vase of water, they will begin to flower, giving you a taste of spring in winter.

FEBRUARY

8

9

Continue to check for insect pests on your houseplants.

10

11

Thoroughly clean empty planters, containers and seed trays to get them ready for spring planting.

12

13

14

Try planting hollyhocks (*left*) together with other tall annuals such as sunflowers and black-eyed Susans for a pretty display at the back of a flowerbed. Petunia (*top right*), bellflower (*far right*) and begonia (*near right*) are plants you can start from seed in February.

Start seeds for annuals, perennials and vegetables that are slow to mature. A few to consider are

- Begonia (*Begonia*)
- Bellflower (*Campanula*)
- Impatiens (*Impatiens*)
- Lady's Mantle (*Alchemilla*)
- Pansy (*Viola*)
- Petunia (*Petunia*)
- Pinks (*Dianthus*)
- Snapdragon (*Antirrhinum*)
- Verbena (*Verbena*)

Starting plants from seed is a great way to propagate a large number of plants at a relatively low cost. You can grow plants you can't find at any garden centre and get a jump-start on the growing season.

FEBRUARY

15

16

Keep seedlings in the brightest location available to reduce stretching.

17

18

Check to see if any of the tubers or bulbs you are storing indoors have started sprouting. Pot them and keep them in a bright location once they do.

19

20

Many varieties of dahlia (*below*) can be started from seed in February for transplanting after the danger of frost has passed. Fresh herbs growing in a greenhouse (*centre right*); seed tray, pots, soil and spray mister for indoor seeding (*bottom right*)

21

As the days start to lengthen, indoor plants may start to show signs of new growth. Increase watering and apply a weak fertilizer (1/4 strength) only after they begin to grow.

Seedlings will be weak and floppy if they don't get enough light. Consider purchasing a fluorescent or other grow light (*above*) to provide extra illumination for them.

STARTING SEEDS

What you will need to start seeds:
- containers to grow them in, such as pots, trays or peat pots
- sterile potting or seed-starting mix
- plastic bags or tray covers to keep the seedbed humid
- a hand-held spray mister and a heating coil or pad (optional).

Tips for growing healthy seedlings:
- Transplant seedlings to individual containers once they have their third true leaf to prevent crowding.
- Space plants so that the leaves do not overshadow those of neighbouring plants.

23

24

After seeds have been planted, and once seedlings emerge, moisten the soil with a hand-held spray mister when the soil begins to dry out.

25

26

Don't fertilize young seedlings. Wait until the seed leaves (the first leaves to appear) have begun to shrivel, then fertilize with a weak fertilizer once a week.

27

28

29

Lupins (*left*) are stately plants sporting lovely fan-shaped leaves and spiky, colourful blooms. Start them indoors in February or March. Lupin seeds have a hard coating, so before seeding, scratch or scrape them to allow moisture to penetrate the seed coat and permit germination.

Tips for starting seeds:

- Moisten the potting mix before you fill the containers.

- Firm the potting mix down in the containers, but don't pack it too tightly.

- Leave seeds that require light for germination uncovered.

- Plant large seeds individually by poking a hole in the potting mix with the tip of a pen or pencil and then dropping the seed in the hole.

- Spread small seeds evenly across the soil surface, then lightly cover with more potting mix.

- To spread small seeds, place them in the crease of a folded piece of paper and gently tap the bottom of the fold to roll them onto the potting mix (*top right*).

- Mix very tiny seeds, like those of begonia, with very fine sand before planting to spread them out more evenly.

- Plant only one type of seed in each container. Some seeds will germinate before others, and it is difficult to keep both seeds and seedlings happy in the same container.

- Cover pots or trays of seeds with clear plastic to keep them moist (*bottom right*).

- Seeds do not need bright, direct light to germinate and can be kept in an out-of-the-way place until they begin to sprout.

- Once the seeds germinate, keep the seedlings in a bright location and remove the plastic cover.

To prevent seedlings from damping-off, always use a sterile potting or soil-less mix, thoroughly clean containers before using them, maintain good air circulation around seedlings and water from the bottom, keeping the soil moist, not soggy.

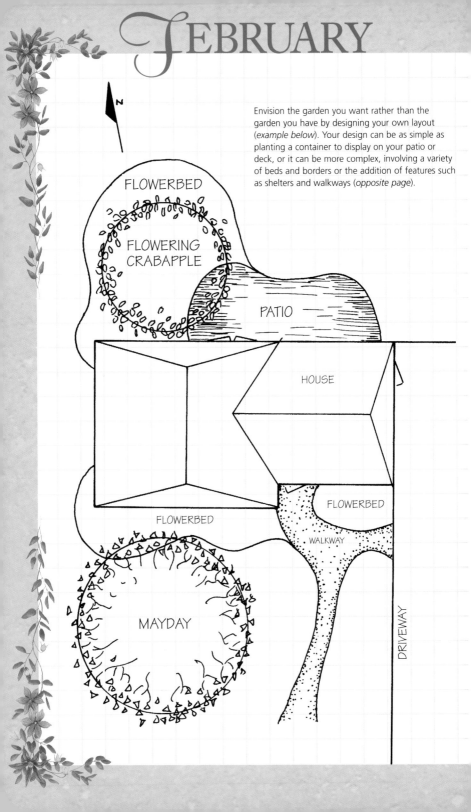

N

FLOWERBED

FLOWERING
CRABAPPLE

PATIO

Envision the garden you want rather than the garden you have by designing your own layout (*example below*). Your design can be as simple as planting a container to display on your patio or deck, or it can be more complex, involving a variety of beds and borders or the addition of features such as shelters and walkways (*opposite page*).

HOUSE

FLOWERBED

FLOWERBED

WALKWAY

MAYDAY

DRIVEWAY

GARDEN PLANNING

Using graph paper, plot out the existing yard and house:

- Analyze your garden for strengths and weaknesses, and identify specific zones in your yard. Create a master plan and then sub-plans so you can keep track of the present situation, problem areas, future needs and any changes you want to make.

- Organize outdoor rooms in the front and back yards, and create sub-plans that focus on different themes, such as vegetable, herb and inspiration gardens.

- If you include a vegetable garden, create a plan to keep track of crop rotations.

- Install trees, shrubs, solid structures and unique accents. Garden beds can be added later if you're not sure where to place them.

March

Weather anomalies abound in March.
Snow blankets the garden one day and starts
to melt the next as spring begins.

MARCH

1

2

Prune trees and shrubs that were damaged over winter.

3

4

The single most important thing you can do when planting is to make sure you have the right plant in the right location. Consider the mature size of the plant and its cultural requirements.

5

6

When designing your garden, consider planting a fast-growing, drought-tolerant elder (*left and near right*). The elder's showy foliage adds colour and texture to a landscape, and its edible berries can be made into jelly or wine or left for the birds. Prune red-twig dogwoods (*top right and far right*) in early spring.

7

W hen warm weather finally arrives, we may feel a little anxious for the gardening season to get under-way, but it is in our garden's best interest to keep plants dormant for just a little longer. Newly emerging plants can be seriously damaged or killed when the weather takes a turn for the worse.

THINGS TO DO

The first few tasks of spring get us out in the garden by late March.

Days can be warm enough to encourage some plants to start sprouting. Keep snow piled on beds or mulches topped up to protect plants from the freezing nights.

MARCH

8

9

As the snow begins to melt, start clearing up the debris in your yard, such as leaves, sticks, garbage and doggie poop.

10

11

Prune late-flowering shrubs (July or later) and shrubs grown for colourful young growth.

12

13

14

As soon as the snow begins to melt in spring, the leaves of bergenia become visible and are quickly followed by its pretty magenta flowers (*left*). Spirea (*top right*); hardy kiwi (*centre right*); hydrangea (*bottom right*)

Keep off your lawn when it is frozen, bare of snow and/or very wet to avoid damaging the grass or compacting the soil.

Apply horticultural oil (also called dormant oil), used to control overwintering insects, to trees, shrubs and vines before the buds swell. Follow the directions carefully to avoid harming beneficial insects.

Plants to prune in early spring:
- Alpine Currant (*Ribes alpinum*)
- Hardy Kiwi (*Actinidia arguta*)
- Hydrangea (*Hydrangea* spp.)
- Japanese Spirea (*Spirea japonica*)
- Potentilla (*Potentilla* spp.)
- Tartarian Dogwood (*Cornus alba*)
- Yellow or Purple-leafed Elders (*Sambucus* spp.)

15

16

Continue indoor seeding. Most of the seeds you may wish to start early can be started by late March.

17

18

Water houseplants that start sprouting new growth more frequently, and apply a weak fertilizer.

19

20

21

Peegee hydrangea (*left*) is a popular and adaptable shrub that grows well in a protected site with moist soil. It is lovely in full bloom. If planted early enough in spring, clematis (*top right*) flowers the first summer; daffodils are among the earliest spring bloomers (*bottom right*).

PLANTING IN SPRING

Soon we'll be heading into prime planting season. As soon as the ground can be cultivated, dormant stock can be planted. Trees, shrubs, vines and perennials often establish most quickly when they are planted just as they are about to break dormancy. They are full of growth hormones, and they recover quickly from transplant shock.

Avoid using dormant oil on blue-needled evergreens, such as blue spruce (*above*). The treatment takes the blue off the existing needles, though the new needles will be blue.

MARCH

22

23

Before doing any digging, call your utility companies to locate any buried wires, cables or pipes to prevent injury and save time and money.

24

25

Don't plant vigorous spreaders in rock gardens with tiny alpine plants or large shrubs right next to walkways.

26

27

28

Cornflowers (*left*) are both pretty and tough. They do well in full sun and poor soil and can survive our winters with little or no protection. Russian sage, coneflower and thread-leaf coreopsis (*top right*); mountain ash (*bottom right*)

A few things to keep in mind when planting your garden:

- Never work with your soil when it is very wet or very dry.
- Avoid planting during the hottest, sunniest part of the day. Choose an overcast day, or plant early or late in the day.
- Prepare your soil before you plant to avoid damaging roots later.
- Get your new plants into the ground as soon as possible when you get them home. Roots can get hot and dry out quickly in containers. Keep plants in a shady spot if you must wait to plant them.
- Most plants are happiest when planted at the same depth they have always grown at. Trees, in particular, can be killed by too deep a planting.
- Remove containers before planting. Plastic and fibre pots restrict root growth and prevent plants from becoming established.
- Plants should be well watered when they are newly planted. Watering deeply and infrequently will encourage the strongest root growth.
- Check the root zone before watering. The soil surface may appear dry when the roots are still moist.

MARCH

29

30

31

If a plant needs well-drained soil and full sun to thrive, it will be healthiest and best able to fight off problems in those conditions. Work with your plants' natural tendencies.

The splendid yellow shrub rose 'Morden Sunrise' (*below*) is one of the few yellow roses hardy enough for prairie gardens.

Harden annuals and perennials off before planting them by gradually exposing them to longer periods of time outside. Doing so gives your plants time to adapt to outdoor weather conditions and reduces the chance of transplant shock.

Remove only damaged branches when planting trees or shrubs, and leave the plant to settle in for at least one year before you begin any formative pruning. Plants need all the branches and leaves they have when they are trying to get established.

Trees less than 1.5 m (5') tall do not need staking unless they are in a very windy location. Unstaked trees develop stronger root systems.

planting a balled-and-burlapped tree

staking a tree properly

planting a bare-root tree

APRIL

Though April can be unpredictable,
we welcome the arrival
of mild spring weather.

APRIL

1

2

Plant trees, shrubs and vines once the soil can be worked.

3

4

Check your power tools, such as the lawn mower, and have them serviced if you didn't do it over winter.

5

6

7

The columbine (*left*) is a beautiful flower that some say resembles a bird in flight. Its jewel-like colours herald the coming of summer. *Clockwise from top right*: primroses, foxgloves, million bells

Visit a garden centre. A diverse selection of uncommon annuals and perennials is sometimes available early. You may also be able to purchase woody plants while they are still dormant. Many garden centres will take your name and call you when the plants you are looking for arrive.

During the first warm days of April, it is easy to forget that cold, frosty nights and late spring snowfalls are still very likely. Spring bulbs are emerging, buds are swelling, plant life is reawakening and summer days are just around the corner. We prairie gardeners require very little in the way of motivation to get our hands in the dirt. Some gardeners may want to start seeding cold-hardy vegetables in pots or in protected areas of their gardens if the ground has thawed and warmed sufficiently. This month offers the perfect opportunity to finish tidying our gardens for the rush of activities that spring is sure to bring.

APRIL

8

9

Repot houseplants if needed.

10

11

12

13

14

Consider planting daylilies (*left*) this spring. Though the blooms last only a day, these lilies are easygoing, prolific and versatile and come in an almost infinite variety of forms, sizes and colours. Sweet peas (*top right*); Iceland poppies (*bottom right*) can be sown directly into the garden in spring; French marigolds (*right*)

THINGS TO DO

The real gardening work begins—raking, digging, planting and pruning. We begin the hard work that will let us sit back and enjoy the garden once summer arrives.

Bring garden tools out of storage and examine them for rust or other damage. Clean and sharpen them if you didn't before you put them away in fall.

Store any plants you have purchased or started indoors in as bright a location as possible. You may begin to harden them off by placing them outdoors for a short period each day.

Avoid working your soil until it has thawed and dried out a bit. A handful of thawed soil should squeeze into a ball that holds its shape but breaks easily apart when pressed with a thumb or finger.

Seeds sown directly into the garden may take longer to germinate than those planted indoors, but the resulting plants will be stronger.

APRIL

15

16

Divide perennials that bloom in mid-summer or later, such as asters, daylilies and sedums.

17

18

Clean up the garden once the snow has melted. Rake debris off lawns and prune back old perennial growth.

19

20

21

A traditional garden favourite, sweet peas (*left*) are easy to grow from seed in spring. They sprout quickly and have sweetly scented blooms that can be cut often for fragrant indoor bouquets. *Clockwise from top right*: phlox, cabbage, rocket larkspur and nigella be planted before the last spring frost.

Warming up vegetable beds with row covers allows many plants and seeds to be sown early.

Many plants prefer to grow in cool weather and can be started well before the last frost. These seeds can be planted as soon as the soil can be worked:

- Bachelor's Buttons (*Centaurea cyanus*)
- Cabbage (*Brassica oleracea*)
- Calendula (*Calendula officinalis*)
- California Poppy (*Eschscholzia californica*)
- Godetia (*Clarkia amoena*)
- Kale (*Brassica napus*)
- Love-in-a-Mist (*Nigella damascena*)
- Peas (*Pisum sativum*)
- Phlox (*Phlox drummondii*)
- Poppy (*Papaver rhoeas*)
- Rocket Larkspur (*Consolida ajacis*)
- Spinach (*Spinacea oleracea*)
- Sweet Pea (*Lathyrus odoratus*)
- Swiss Chard (*Beta vulgaris*)

APRIL

22

23

Pull back mulch from sprouting plants on warm days, but be prepared to cover plants back over on cold nights.

24

25

Tomatoes, snapdragons and spiderflowers can be started from seed only a few weeks before moving them into the garden.

26

27

28

You can depend on aubrieta (*left*) to put on a great floral show in spring. *Clockwise from top right*: spiral juniper; pom-pom juniper; pineapple-shaped arborvitae

PRUNING

Prune trees and shrubs to maintain the health and attractive shape of a plant, increase the quality and yield of fruit, control and direct growth and create interesting plant forms and shapes.

Once you learn how to prune plants correctly, it is an enjoyable garden task. There are many good books available on the topic of pruning. One is listed at the back of this book. If you are unsure about pruning, take a pruning course, often offered by garden centres, botanical gardens and adult education courses.

Don't prune trees or shrubs when growth has started and buds are swelling. Prune before growth starts in spring or wait until plants have leafed out. Don't prune off the tops of your trees. Topping damages tree health.

Clockwise from top right: climbing rose with support; espaliered apple tree; proper secateur orientation

PRUNING TIPS

- Prune at the right time of year. Trees and shrubs that flower before June, usually on the previous year's wood, should be pruned after they have flowered. Trees and shrubs that flower after June, usually on new growth, can be pruned in spring.

- Use the correct tool for the size of branch to be removed: secateurs, or hand pruners, for growth up to 2 cm (3/4") in diameter; long-handled loppers for growth up to 4 cm (1 1/2") in diameter; or a pruning saw for growth up to about 15 cm (6") in diameter.

- Always use sterile, sharp tools.

- Always use secateurs or loppers with the blade side towards the plant and the hook towards the part to be removed.

thinning cuts

Thin trees and shrubs to promote the growth of younger, healthier branches. Doing so rejuvenates a plant.

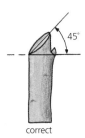

45°

correct | too low | angle too great | too high

When pruning, avoid the following:

- Don't leave stubs. Whether you are cutting off a large branch or deadheading a lilac, always cut back to a join. Branches should be removed to the branch collar, and smaller growth should be cut back to a bud or branch union. There is no absolute set angle for pruning. Each plant should be pruned according to its individual needs.

- Never use pruning paint or paste. Trees have a natural ability to create a barrier between living and dead wood. Painting over a cut impairs this ability.

- Never try to remove a tree or large branch by yourself. Have someone help you, or hire a professional to do it.

Always hire an ISA (International Society of Arboriculture) certified professional to remove branches on trees growing near power lines or other hazardous areas, especially if they could damage a building, fence or car if they were to fall. Do not for any reason prune elms between April 1 and July 31. Pruning at this time spreads Dutch elm disease.

MAY

As buds and blooms begin
to emerge, May brings us hope that
winter is now behind us.

MAY

1

2

Move or divide any perennials that didn't have enough space last summer.

3

4

Prune early-flowering shrubs, such as forsythia, once they are finished flowering, if needed.

5

6

7

The Japanese anemone or windflower (*left*) is a delight in spring and fall, when it puts on a charming floral display. Fragrant lilacs (*top right*) are hard to resist; mayday trees (*bottom right*) are among the first trees to leaf out and bloom in spring on the prairies.

May weather can still be unpredictable, one year warm and sunny, the next frosty and threatening flurries. In a typical May, bulbs bloom, peonies poke up their red and green spears and forsythias and lilacs burst forth in a riot of yellow and purple.

THINGS TO DO

A new gardening season awaits, one where we haven't forgotten to weed or water, where all our plants are properly spaced and well staked and where no insects have chewed any leaves. Now is the time to finish tidying up the garden, prepare the garden beds and get the planting done.

It is vital to keep plants well watered when they are breaking dormancy to prevent new shoots from drying out.

MAY

8

9

*Begin to harden off any houseplants you
plan to move outdoors for summer.*

10

11

*Work compost into your garden beds
and fork them over, removing weeds
as you go, to prepare them for planting
later in the month.*

12

13

14

Clematis such as C. 'Gravetye Beauty' (*left*) is a
popular perennial vine with beautiful, showy flowers
in many shapes and sizes. By planting a variety of
them, you can have clematis in bloom from spring
to fall. *Clockwise from top right*: C. 'Hagley hybrid';
C. *integrifolia*; C. 'Etoile Violette'

Remove mulch from perennials and trim back and clear away any of last year's growth if it was still too cold to do so in April.

Clear away any of the annuals or vegetables that didn't make it to the compost pile last fall.

By the end of the month, you will have a good idea of what has been damaged or killed back over winter, and you can trim or remove plants as needed.

Accept that grass will not grow everywhere. Grass requires plenty of sun and regular moisture. Many trees and buildings provide too much shade and don't allow enough water to penetrate the soil for grass to grow successfully. Use mulch or other groundcovers in areas where you have trouble growing grass. When selecting trees to plant in the lawn, choose ones that will provide only light shade and that will enjoy the plentiful water they will be sharing with the grass, or have a grass-free zone extending from the base of the tree to the dripline.

MAY

15

16

*Continue to harden off your early-started
seedlings and purchased plants so they
will be ready to plant outside when the
weather is warm enough.*

17

18

*When planning your vegetable garden,
consider planting extra to donate
to a local food bank or homeless shelter.*

19

20

21

Plant a sunny spring flower such as
doronicum (*left*) with tulips and
forget-me-nots to create a cheerful
May display.

It is possible to have a healthy, attractive organic lawn. Grass is an extremely competitive plant, capable of fighting off invasions by weeds, pests and diseases without the use of chemicals.

Lawns need very little water to remain green. Watering deeply and infrequently will encourage deep roots that are not easily damaged during periods of drought. Five millimetres (1/4") of water a week will keep grass alive and 2.5 cm (1") a week will keep it green (*below*).

The last spring frost for our province usually has occurred by May 24, but don't restrict yourself to planting only after this date. Judge the planting by how the year is progressing. In a warm year, when nights stay above freezing even early in the month, it is worth putting in a few tender plants such as tomatoes. If there are no more frosts, you will have gained several weeks on our short growing season. In a cool year you may have to wait until early June before planting tender heat-lovers, such as beans (*left*), to give the soil more time to warm up.

MAY

22

23

*Start new garden beds or expand
and improve old ones.*

24

25

*De-thatch lawns in spring only when the
thatch layer is more than 2 cm (3/4") deep.*

26

27

28

Despite their exotic appearance,
hostas (*left*) flourish in prairie
gardens. A wide variety will grow
and thrive here in light shade and
rich, moist soil.

TURFGRASS

Turfgrass aficionados are having a hard time these days. Cities across Canada are taking steps to ban pesticide use on lawns, and summer water bans leave turf dry and crisp during hot spells. Alternative groundcovers and xeriscapes are being hailed as the way of the future, but there are positives to turfgrasses that make them worth keeping. Lawns efficiently filter pollutants out of run-off water, prevent soil erosion, retain moisture, cool the air and resist drought.

Although lawns require a layer of thatch to improve wear tolerance, reduce compaction and insulate against weather extremes, too thick a thatch layer can prevent water absorption, make the grass susceptible to heat, drought and cold and encourage pest and disease problems.

May-blooming flowers: (*clockwise from top*) bearded irises bloom in early spring; lily-of-the-valley is a spring bloomer with scented flowers; phlox flowers attract bees and butterflies in spring and look exceptional in rock gardens.

MAY

29

30

May is the perfect time to plant such vegetables as beans, beets, leaf lettuce, peas, potatoes, radishes and spinach. They are easy to grow from seed and mature quickly.

31

Forget-me-nots (*left*), rockcress (*aubrieta*) (*top right*) and bergenia (*bottom right*) are easy-to-grow, reliable bloomers and perfect for beginner gardeners.

Here are some tips for maintaining a healthy, organic lawn:

- Aerate your lawn in spring, after active growth begins, to relieve compaction and allow water and air to move freely through the soil.

- Feed the soil, not the plants. Organic fertilizers or compost will encourage a healthy population of soil microbes. These work with roots to provide plants with nutrients and to fight off attacks by pests and diseases. Apply an organic fertilizer in late spring after you aerate the lawn and in fall just as the grass goes dormant.

- Mow lawns to a height of 5 to 6 cm (2–2¹⁄₂"). If kept this height, the remaining blade will shade the ground, preventing moisture loss,

keeping roots cooler, reducing the stress the grass suffers from being mowed and helping the grass out-compete weeds for space and sunlight.

- Grass clippings should be left on the lawn to return their nutrients to the soil and add organic matter. Mowing your lawn once a week or as often as needed during the vigorous growing season will ensure that the clippings decompose quickly.

- Healthy turfgrass will out-compete most weeds. Remove weeds by hand. If you must use chemicals, apply them only to the weeds. Chemical herbicides disrupt the balance of soil microbes and are not necessary to have a healthy lawn.

JUNE

A striking palette of colour explodes
against a lush green backdrop.
Summer has officially arrived.

JUNE

1

2

Plant tender transplants such as pumpkins, tomatoes, begonias and coleus.

3

4

Heat-loving plants such as beans and marigolds will germinate quickly in the warm soil. Direct sow early in June.

5

6

7

Cranesbill geraniums (*left*) are charming late spring perennial flowers with attractive foliage. Use them to hide the bases of larger shrubs and perennials. Petunias (*top right*) look great in beds, baskets and planters; daylilies (*bottom right*) planted en masse serve as a screen.

In June, the grass is green, flowerbeds flourish and drifts of perennials continue to bloom while trees and shrubs thrive. We watch as seeds germinate and tiny plants emerge. Last frosts are generally over, and the soil is warm enough for even the tenderest plants. Rain is usually plentiful in June, but in a dry year, newly planted annuals and perennials may need supplemental watering until they become established.

THINGS TO DO

June is the month to finish up the planting and begin the general maintenance work that will keep larger projects to a minimum.

Stake plants before they fill in if you haven't already done so.

Apply mulch to shrub, perennial and vegetable beds. Doing so will shade the roots and reduce the amount of water the plants will require.

Pinch late-flowering perennials back lightly to encourage bushier growth and more flowers.

If you haven't done so already, clean out your water garden.

Remove dead flowers from plants growing in tubs, window-boxes and hanging baskets. Deadheading encourages more flowering and keeps displays looking tidy.

JUNE

8

9

Prune early-flowering shrubs and perennials when they are finished blooming.

10

11

Identify the insects you find in your garden. You may be surprised to find out how many are beneficial.

12

13

14

Catmint (*left*) has many virtues: it's an edible herb, it works well in a variety of garden settings, it blooms from spring to fall and it's virtually pest and disease free. Clockwise from top: bee balm, black-eyed Susan mixed with purple coneflower; artemesia; godetia

Perennials to pinch back in June:
- Artemisia (*Artemisia* species)
- Bee Balm (*Monarda didyma*)
- Black-eyed Susan (*Rudbeckia* species)
- Catmint (*Nepeta* hybrids)
- Purple Coneflower (*Echinacea purpurea*)
- Shasta Daisy (*Leucanthemum* hybrids)

JUNE

Pull weeds out of beds when you see them to avoid having to spend an entire day doing it later.

Water transplants regularly until they become established.

Coreopsis (*left*) enlivens a summer garden with its bright yellow, continuous blooms. Shear back in late summer for more flowers in fall. *Clockwise from top right*: flowering maple (*abutilon*) can be grown in a container outdoors in summer and kept as a houseplant in winter; charming container garden display of impatiens, marigolds and geraniums; million bells with bidens

CONTAINER GARDENING

Most plants can be grown in containers. Annuals, perennials, vegetables, shrubs and even trees can be adapted to container culture.

There are many advantages to gardening in containers:

- They work well in small spaces. Even apartment dwellers with small balconies can enjoy the pleasures of gardening with planters on the balcony.

- They are mobile. Containers can be moved around to take advantage of light or shade and can even be moved into a sheltered location for winter.

- They are easier to reach. Container plantings allow people in wheelchairs or with back problems to garden without having to do a lot of bending.

- They are useful for extending the season. Many plants require a longer growing season than we experience on the prairies. You can get an early start without the transplant shock that many plants suffer when moved outdoors.

JUNE

22

23

Put trailing plants near the edge of a container to spill out and bushy and upright plants in the middle where they will give height and depth to the planting.

24

25

Consider mixing different plants together in a container. You can create contrasts of colour, texture and habit and give a small garden an inviting appearance.

26

27

28

The flowers of *Salvia farinacea* 'Victoria' (*left*) are a beautiful deep violet blue. They look stunning planted with yellow or orange flowers such as nasturtiums, California poppies or marigolds. *Opposite page*: some examples of attractive container gardens

Gardeners can get more than a month's head start on the gardening season by using containers. Tomatoes, pumpkins and watermelons can be started from seed in April. Planted in large containers, they can be moved outside during warm days and brought back in at night for most of May. Doing so prevents the stretching that many early-started plants suffer from if kept indoors for too long before being planted in the garden.

Many houseplants enjoy spending summer outside in a shady location. The brighter a location you provide for your plant indoors, the more likely it is to do well outdoors. Avoid putting plants in direct sun, though, because they will have a hard time adjusting to the intensity of the light and to the lack of light when they are moved back indoors at the end of summer.

JUNE

29

30

Keep an eye open for the early signs of pest and disease problems. They are easiest to deal with when they are just beginning.

Over the winter, shelter your container plants from the damaging effects of the wind and sun. Container soil must remain frozen until plants break dormancy in spring or their roots may be damaged.

Though considered old-fashioned by some gardeners, petunias (*below*) are versatile and dependable annuals that bloom continuously in any sunny location. New varieties of this flower seem to appear every spring in prairie greenhouses. Spirea (*top right*) by water feature

Water gardens can be created in containers. Many ready-made container gardens are available, or you can create your own. Garden centres have lots of water garden supplies, and many water plants will grow as well in a large tub as they will in a pond.

Most perennials, shrubs and trees will require more winter protection in containers than they would if grown in the ground. Because the roots are above ground level, they are exposed to the winter wind and cycles of freezing and thawing. Protect container-grown plants by insulating the inside of the container. Sheets of foam insulation can be purchased and fit around the inside of the pot before the soil is added. Containers can also be moved to sheltered locations. Garden sheds and unheated garages work well to protect plants from the elements, but remember to water your containers thoroughly until the soil freezes, and also if the soil thaws out before spring, to keep roots moist.

Prune evergreens when new growth is still tender and has fully extended (*right*). Pinch back by up to half to encourage bushier growth. Never cut evergreens back into old wood—most can't regenerate from old wood.

JULY

Spring's frantic pace slows to
July's gentle rhythms. Sit back and enjoy
the fruits of your labours.

JULY

1

2

Deadhead repeat-blooming annuals and perennials regularly to keep them looking their best.

3

4

Cut flowers to use in fresh arrangements indoors.

5

6

7

'Morden Fireglow' (*left*) is an ideal shrub rose for our climate. Its scarlet double blooms, fresh scent and self cleaning habit make it a prairie favourite. A riot of phlox, daylilies, yarrow, blue sage and snapdragons (*top right*); barberry (*bottom right*)

Flowerbeds that were sparse are now dense and rich with colour. Bushels of beans are ready to be picked, and green tomatoes begin to ripen on the vine. The season's transplants are now established and require less frequent watering.

With our long, warm days and short, cool nights, plants grow at a rapid and prolific pace. Those blessed with longer growing seasons are astonished to discover what we can grow here. Never underestimate the power of long growing days.

THINGS TO DO

Heat and drought can spell disaster for your lawn and garden if you haven't followed good watering practices. Water bans are common in communities all across Canada, and frequent, shallow watering earlier in the season makes for problems in July when roots unaccustomed to searching deeply for water suffer in its absence.

Water deeply, but no more than once a week during dry spells. Water early in the day to minimize potential disease and reduce water lost through evaporation.

Top up water gardens regularly if levels drop because of evaporation.

JULY

8

9

Weed regularly to keep beds tidy.

10

11

Turn the compost pile and when the compost is ready, add it to your flowerbeds and vegetable garden.

12

13

14

Salvia (*left*) loves sun, and its brilliantly coloured flowers attract butterflies and hummingbirds to the garden. Plant it among other sun-loving annuals and perennials where its bright reds, oranges, pinks and purples will provide bright bursts of colour.
Clockwise from top right: violas; statice; bachelor's buttons

Thin vegetable crops such as beets, carrots and turnips. Crowded plants lead to poor crops.

Use an organic liquid fertilizer on container plants and on garden plants if compost is scarce.

Pick zucchini when they are small. They are tender and tasty and you are less likely to wind up with boxes full of foot-long zucchini to leave on unsuspecting neighbours' front doorsteps. Consider donating extra vegetables to a homeless shelter or food bank, where they will be much appreciated.

Plan to replace fading flowers and vegetables by sowing seeds for a fall display or crop. Peas, bush beans, annual candytuft and lobelia are often finished fruiting or blooming by mid- to late summer, leaving holes in the garden that can be filled by new plants. Seeds for replacement plants can be direct sown or started indoors.

JULY

15

16

Top up mulch if it gets thin in places in your garden. Mulch protects roots and helps keep weeds at bay.

17

18

Continue to tie plants to their stakes as they grow.

19

20

Heliopsis (*left*), a native prairie perennial, is easy to grow and tolerates poor conditions, though it thrives in full sun and fertile, moist soil. Its name means "resembling the sun" and its sun-like blooms make long-lasting cut flowers. Use a mixture of annuals and perennials to create garden rooms that add privacy or create paths through the garden (*opposite page*).

21

Plants survive and flourish in environments that best meet their needs. Determine the ideal growing conditions for your flowers, trees and shrubs, and then plant them where these conditions exist in your yard. A plant that needs good drainage and full sun, for example, will never do well in a boggy, north-facing location.

GARDEN PROBLEMS

Problems such as chewed leaves, mildews and nutrient deficiencies tend to become noticeable in July when plants finish their first flush of growth and turn their attention to flowering and fruiting.

Such problems can be minimized if you develop a good problem management program. Though it may seem complicated, problem management is a simple process that relies on correct and timely identification of the problem and then using the least environmentally harmful method to deal with it.

JULY

22

23

Prune shrubs that have finished flowering to encourage the development of young shoots that will bear flowers the following year.

24

25

Trim hedges regularly to keep them looking tidy and lush.

26

27

28

'Cupcake' (*left*) is a delightful miniature rose with a classic hybrid tea shape. It produces an abundance of blooms and is disease resistant. *Clockwise from top right*: deerpruned cedars; a swallowtail on cherry blossoms; a birdbath in a shade garden

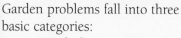

Garden problems fall into three
basic categories:

- pests, including insects such as
  aphids, nematodes and whiteflies,
  and animals such as mice, rabbits
  and deer

- diseases, caused by bacteria,
  fungi and viruses

- physiological problems, caused
  by nutrient deficiencies, too
  much or too little water and
  incorrect light levels.

Choose healthy plants that have
been developed for their resistance
to common problems and that will
perform well in the conditions pro-
vided by your garden.

Prevention is the most
important aspect of problem
management. A healthy
garden is resistant to problems
and develops a natural
balance between beneficial
and detrimental organisms.

JULY

29

30

Neem oil is a natural insecticide that is becoming more popular with gardeners. It can kill a wide range of pests, and it is completely safe for residential use.

31

Cup-and-saucer vine (*below*) produces sweetly scented flowers that are cream coloured when they emerge and turn purple as they age. Ladybug (*top right*), a beneficial insect that feasts on aphids; Dahlberg daisies (*bottom right*)

PEST CONTROL

Correct identification of problems is the key to solving them. Just because an insect is on a plant doesn't mean it's doing any harm.

Chemical pest control should always be a last resort. There are many alternatives that pose no danger to gardeners or their families and pets.

- Cultural controls are the day-to-day gardening techniques you use to keep your garden healthy. Weeding, mulching, keeping tools clean and growing problem-resistant cultivars are a few techniques you can use to keep gardens healthy.

- Physical controls are the hands-on part of problem solving. Picking insects off leaves, removing diseased foliage and creating barriers to stop rabbits from getting into the vegetable patch are examples of physical controls.

- Biological controls use natural and introduced populations of parasites or predators that prey on pests. Birds, snakes, frogs, spiders, some insects and even bacteria naturally feed on some problem insects. Soil microbes work with plant roots to increase their resistance to disease.

The pesticide industry has responded to consumer demand for effective, environmentally safe pest control products. Biopesticides are made from plant, animal, bacterial or mineral sources. They are effective in small quantities and decompose quickly in the environment. These products may reduce our reliance on chemical pesticides.

AUGUST

The warm summer days continue,
but as the garden ripens,
nature reminds us that fall is near.

AUGUST

1

2

Reduce fertilizer applications to allow perennials, shrubs and trees ample time to harden off before the cold weather.

3

4

Continue to water during dry spells. Plants shouldn't need deep watering more than once a week at this time of the year.

5

6

7

Calendula (*left*) is an easy flower to grow from seed. It blooms quickly in spring and all summer long, even tolerating light frost. It can be used as a culinary herb as well. *Clockwise from top right:* borage; Nanking cherry; petunias

As the days become shorter, the nights grow cooler. Solid greens slowly transform into warm, fiery hues. Fall frosts are imminent in late August in some areas.

THINGS TO DO

Gardeners consider August a jewel. We can finally put down our tools and sit back and enjoy ourselves. Little else is left to do but tie up floppy flower spikes, harvest fruit and vegetables and remove the odd weed. The manic days of summer have come and gone and a lazy fall awaits.

Continue to deadhead perennials and annuals to keep the blooms coming.

Remove worn-out annuals and vegetables, and replace them with the ones you started last month. Shearing some annuals and perennials back will encourage new growth, giving them a fresh look for fall.

Keep an eye open for pests that may be planning to hibernate in the debris around your plants or the bark of your trees. Taking care of a few insects now may keep several generations out of your garden next summer.

Pick apples as soon as they are ready, being careful not to bruise the fruit.

ᴀUGUST

8

9

Seed areas of lawn that are thin or dead.
The cool weather encourages fast growth. Keep
the seed well watered while it germinates.

10

11

Depending on the size of your perennials,
you can divide them using a shovel or
pitchfork (for large plants), a sharp knife
(for small plants) or your hands
(for easily divided plants).

12

13

14

The French marigold (*left*) is just
one variety of this popular
annual. All marigolds are low-
maintenance plants that stand up
well to heat, wind and rain.

PLANT PROPAGATION

Now is a good time to divide some perennials that have finished blooming and to note which of your plants will need dividing next spring. Look for these signs that perennials need dividing:

- The centre of the plant has died out.
- The plant is no longer flowering as profusely as it did in previous years.
- The plant is encroaching on the growing space of other plants.

August is a good time to propagate plants. Taking cuttings and gathering seed are great ways to increase your plant collection and to share some of your favourite plants with friends and family.

Prairie-hardy species such as Siberian bugloss (*top*), anenome (*top right*), lupin (*centre*) and liatris (*right*) are good plants to divide if you're just starting your perennial collection. All are drought tolerant, especially important on the often-dry prairies.

AUGUST

15

16

Gradually move houseplants that have been summering outdoors into shadier locations so they will be prepared for the lower light levels indoors. Make sure they aren't infested with bugs; the pests will be harder to control once the plants are indoors.

17

18

Turn the layers of the compost pile and continue to add garden soil, kitchen scraps and garden debris that isn't diseased or infested with insects.

19

20

Zinnias (*below*) are easy to grow, come in a rainbow of colours and make long-lasting cut flowers for floral arrangements. *Clockwise from top right*: spirea and cottage pinks, sedum and aster are easy to propagate from stem cuttings.

21

Perennials, trees, shrubs and tender perennials that are treated like annuals can all be started from cuttings. This method is an excellent way to propagate varieties and cultivars that you really like but that are slow or difficult to start from seed or that don't produce viable seed.

The easiest cuttings to take from woody plants such as trees, shrubs and vines are called semi-ripe, semi-mature or semi-hardwood cuttings. They are taken from mature new growth that has not become completely woody yet, usually in late summer or early fall.

There is some debate over what size cuttings should be. Some claim that smaller cuttings are more likely to root and will root more quickly. Others claim that larger cuttings develop more roots and become established more quickly once planted. Try different sizes and see what works best for you.

AUGUST

22

23

Continue watering newly planted perennials, trees and shrubs. Water deeply to encourage root growth.

24

25

Avoid pruning rust-prone plants such as mountain ash and crabapple in late summer and fall because many rusts are releasing spores now.

26

27

28

Start collecting seeds from your borage plants (*left*) in August for planting next season. *Clockwise from top right*: evening primrose; nasturtiums with creeping Jenny; zinnias

The easiest way to start is to collect seeds of annual plants in your own garden. Choose plants that are not hybrids or the seeds will probably not come true to type and may not germinate at all. A few easy plants to collect from are

- Borage (*Borago officinalis*)
- Calendula (*Calendula officinalis*)
- Coriander (*Coriandrum sativum*)
- Evening Primrose (*Oenothera fruticosa*)
- Fennel (*Foeniculum vulgare*)
- Marigold (*Tagetes* species and hybrids)
- Nasturtium (*Tropaeolum majus*)
- Poppy (*Papaver rhoeas*)
- Zinnia (*Zinnia elegans*)

Always make cuttings just below a leaf node, the point where the leaves are attached to the stem.

Many gardeners enjoy the hobby of collecting and planting seed. You need to know a few basic things before you begin:

- Know your plant. Correctly identify the plant and learn about its life cycle. You will need to know when it flowers, when the seeds are likely to ripen and how the plant disperses its seeds in order to collect them.
- Find out if there are special requirements for starting the seeds. For example, do they need a hot or cold period to germinate?

29

30

*Find a source of straw for mulch
now because it can be harder
to find later in fall.*

31

Nasturtiums (*below*) are versatile annuals. Their edible
flowers and foliage are attractive additions to baskets
and containers as well as to salads. Even the seedpods
can be pickled and used as a substitute for capers.
Clockwise from top right: drying poppy seedheads;
Oriental poppy; golden clematis seedheads and flowers

When collecting seed, consider the following:

- Collect seeds once they are ripe but before they are shed from the parent plant.
- Remove capsules, heads or pods as they begin to dry and remove the seeds later, once they are completely dry.
- Place a paper bag over a seed-head as it matures and loosely tie it in place to collect seeds as they are shed.
- Dry seeds after they've been collected. Place them on a paper-lined tray and leave them in a warm, dry location for one to three weeks.
- Separate seeds from the other plant parts before storing.
- Store seeds in air-tight containers in a cool, frost-free location.

Don't collect seeds or plants from the wild because wild harvesting is severely depleting many plant populations. Many species and populations of wild plants are protected, and it is illegal to collect their seeds.

Collecting and saving seeds is a time-honoured tradition. Early settlers brought seeds with them when they came here and saved them carefully each fall for the following spring.

SEPTEMBER

*Summer makes a hasty escape,
but we still have time to celebrate the
garden's last weeks of colour.*

SEPTEMBER

1

2

*Pull out annual plants and vegetables
as they fade or are killed by frost.*

3

4

*Plant colourful fall ornamentals, such
as chrysanthemums, flowering cabbage
and flowering kale, available in
fall at most garden centres.*

5

6

7

Strawflower (*left*), amaranthus and goldenrod (*far
right*) can be harvested now for dried flower
arrangements. Create new kinds of visual
interest in your garden by planting ornamental grasses (*right*), which
come in a wide variety of
heights, shapes and colours.
Those not hardy to our
climate can be used as
annuals.

In September, most gardens experience the first fall frosts, but many annuals will continue to bloom unblemished until the first hard freeze. The leaves have begun to change colour, ripening seedheads emerge and brightly coloured berries and fruit adorn a variety of woody ornamentals.

THINGS TO DO

Having enjoyed another summer garden, your big fall clean-up begins.

Take advantage of end-of-season sales. Many garden centres are getting rid of trees, shrubs and perennials at reduced prices. There is still plenty of time for the roots to become established before the ground freezes. Do not buy plants that are excessively pot bound.

Consider starting some herb seeds now. You can plant them in pots and keep them in a bright window so you'll have fresh herbs to add to soups and salads over winter. Moving herb plants in from outdoors is also possible, but the plants often have a difficult time adapting to the lower light levels indoors.

SEPTEMBER

8

9

After a hard frost, dig up tuberous tender plants such as begonias for drying and storing over winter.

10

11

Continue to water the garden during dry spells. Consistent watering in fall helps prepare plants for winter.

12

13

14

Lilies (*left*) are long-lived, easy-to-grow perennials. They look superb in floral arrangements combined with flowers such as baby's breath (*left*). *Clockwise from top right*: the fall colours and features of Virginia creeper, burning bush, viburnum (highbush cranberry) and sumac

If you've let your weeds get out of hand over summer, be sure to pull them up before they set seed to avoid having even more weeds popping up in the garden next summer.

Cool fall weather is ideal for sowing grass seed and repairing thin patches in the lawn.

So many of our trees and shrubs turn shades of yellow, gold and orange in the fall that it really turns our heads when we see a brilliant red. A good selection of hardy plants consistently turns bright red in fall.

A few examples are
- Amur Maple (*Acer ginnala*)
- Highbush Cranberry (*Viburnum trilobum*)
- Peking Cotoneaster (*Cotoneaster lucidus*)
- Virginia Creeper (*Parthenocissus quinquefolia*)
- Winged Burning Bush (*Euonymus alatus*)

SEPTEMBER

15

16

*Set up birdfeeders and begin to feed
the birds if you didn't do so all summer.*

17

18

*Move tender container plants into a
sheltered location when frost is
expected. This strategy will allow you
to enjoy them for longer.*

19

20

The cheery golden marguerite daisy plant (*below*)
forms a tidy mound that works wonderfully in both
formal and informal garden settings.*Clockwise from
top right*: lilies; tulips with hosta; grape hyacinth
(*Muscari*); rudbeckia (black-eyed Susan)

21

Begin to plant bulbs for a great display next spring. Tulips, daffodils, crocuses, scillas, muscaris and alliums are just a few of the bulbs whose flowers will welcome you back into the garden next year.

Spring-flowering perennials such as primroses and candy-tuft will be a delightful sight come April and May.

For vivacious colour from summer through fall, a continuously blooming perennial such as rudbeckia can't be beat.

SEPTEMBER

22

23

When planting bulbs, don't forget to add a little bonemeal to the soil to encourage root development.

24

25

Check houseplants for insect pests before moving them back indoors for winter.

26

27

28

Echinacea purpurea (*left*), commonly called purple coneflower and used as a popular herbal cold remedy, is a long-blooming, drought-resistant perennial. Its distinctively cone-shaped flowers look good in fresh and dried floral arrangements. *Opposite page*: Garden features such as birdbaths, bird feeders and tall flowering perennials such as bee balm, coneflower and yarrow attract wildlife to your yard.

CREATING WILDLIFE HABITAT

The rapid rate of urban sprawl has led to the relentless expansion of large cities and a loss of habitat for wildlife. Our gardens can easily provide some of the space, shelter, food and water that wildlife needs. Though we may not want to attract every creature, we can make at least some wildlife welcome in our gardens. Here are a few tips for attracting wildlife to your garden:

- Include at least some locally native plants because birds and small mammals are accustomed to eating these plants. Once attracted to your garden, animals may also sample the non-native plants.

- Provide a source of water. A pond with a shallow side or a birdbath will offer water for drinking and bathing. Frogs and toads eat a wide variety of insect pests and will happily take up residence in or near a ground-level water feature.

- A variety of birdfeeders and seed will encourage different species of birds to visit your garden. Some birds will visit an elevated feeder, but others prefer a feeder set at or near ground level. Fill your feeders regularly—once you start to feed the birds, they will expect to find food in your feeders all the time.

29

30

The zinnia (*below*) is named after Johann Gottfried Zinn (1727–59), a German botany professor who first grew a South American zinnia from seed.
Clockwise from top right: birdfeeder; monarda with butterfly; sunflower; maple tree

- Butterflies, hummingbirds and a wide variety of predatory insects will be attracted if you include lots of pollen-producing plants in your garden. Plants such as golden-rod, comfrey, bee balm, salvia, Joe-Pye weed, black-eyed Susan, catmint, purple coneflower, core-opsis, hollyhock and yarrow will attract pollen lovers.
- Shelter is the final aspect to keeping your resident wildlife happy. Patches of dense shrubs, tall grasses and mature trees provide shelter. As well, you can leave a small pile of twiggy brush in an out-of-the-way place. Nature stores and many garden centres sell toad houses and birdhouses.

Inevitably squirrels and chipmunks will try to get at your birdfeeders. Instead of trying to get rid of them, why not leave peanuts and seeds out for them as well? Place them near a tree, where they can easily get at them. If you have a large spruce tree, they will eat the seeds out of the cones. Leave cones out with the other food offerings. The little cone scales that are left when they are done make great mulch for the garden or can be used to prevent slipping on icy walks and driveways.

OCTOBER

Brightly coloured fruits adorn bare branches, marking the inevitable end of summer. Only the strong and well protected will survive autumn's grip.

OCTOBER

1

2

Continue to plant bulbs. They need to get a bit of root growth in fall in order to survive winter.

3

4

Continue to mow the lawn, but don't mow frozen blades of grass. Wait for frost to melt off and dry before cutting the grass.

5

6

7

If the first frost hasn't yet arrived and your apples are still on the tree (*left*), now is the time to harvest them. Some varieties taste better after the first frost, however. *Clockwise from top right*: fall garden scene; a bountiful harvest of carrots; endearing teddy bear sunflowers

The garden has been put to bed, early morning frosts dust fallen leaves and snow tries to fall from the sky. Gardeners take nothing for granted. Warm October days are like gold because we know how cold it will soon be.

THINGS TO DO

October is the time to finish tidying up in preparation for another year.

Harvest any remaining vegetables. Soft fruit such as tomatoes and zucchini should have been harvested before the first frost, but cool-weather vegetables such as carrots, cabbage, brussels sprouts, parsnips and turnips can wait until October because they are frost hardy.

Unless your plants have been afflicted with some sort of disease, you can leave faded perennial growth in place and clean it up in spring. The stems will collect leaves and snow, protecting the roots and crown of the plant over the winter.

OCTOBER

8

9

Continue to tidy up dead plant material. Most can be composted, but diseased material is better thrown out.

10

11

Start mulching the garden, but avoid covering plants completely until the ground has frozen. Doing so prevents plants from rotting and deters small rodents from digging down and feasting on plant roots and crowns.

12

13

14

The leaves of the evergreen groundcover kinnikinnick (*left*), a native prairie plant, turn a lovely bronze-red in fall. The berries are a source of food for birds and other wildlife.

Fall is a great time to improve your soil. Amendments added now can be worked in lightly. By planting time next spring, the amendments will have been further worked in by the actions of worms and other soil microorganisms and by the freezing and thawing that takes place over winter.

When raking up leaves in fall, you can use them in different ways: add them to the compost pile; gather them into their own compost pile to decompose into leaf mould; or mow them over and then pile them onto flowerbeds. Whole leaves can become matted together, encouraging fungal rot.

Local farmers' markets are often the best places to find a wide variety of seasonal vegetables and flowers (*above and below*).

15

16

Continue to water trees and shrubs deeply until freeze up. Apply an anti-desiccant or provide a burlap screen to protect newly planted shrubs and evergreens, but avoid completely wrapping plants up in burlap or other materials.

17

18

After raking, and once the lawn is dormant, apply an organic fertilizer. If you haven't needed to mow in a couple of weeks, it is probably sufficiently dormant.

19

20

21

Honeysuckle vine (*left*) flowers from summer to fall frost. Prune in spring to cut back dead growth as new leaves emerge. Composting (*far right*); delicious vegetables harvested from the garden (*near right*)

COMPOSTING

One of the best additives for any type of soil is compost. Compost can be purchased at most garden centres, and many communities now have composting programs. You can easily make compost in your own garden. Though garden refuse and vegetable scraps from your kitchen left in a pile will eventually decompose, it is possible to produce compost more quickly. Here are a few suggestions for creating compost:

- Compost decomposes most quickly when there is a balance between dry and fresh materials. There should be more dry matter, such as chopped straw or shredded leaves, than green matter, such as vegetable scraps and grass clippings.
- Layer the dry and the green matter and mix in some garden soil or previously finished compost. This step introduces decomposer organisms to the pile.

OCTOBER

22

23

As outdoor gardening winds down, try starting bulbs such as paperwhites (narcissus) indoors. Fragrant white blooms should emerge in a few weeks.

24

25

Cure winter squash, such as pumpkins, acorn squash and spaghetti squash, in a cool, frost-free location before storing for winter.

26

27

28

Yarrow's showy, flat-topped flower-heads (*left*) provide months of continuous colour in summer and persist into winter.

- Compost won't decompose properly if it is too wet or too dry. Keep the pile covered during heavy rain and sprinkle it with water if it is too dry. The correct level of moisture can best be described as that of a wrung-out sponge.

- To aerate the pile, use a garden fork to poke holes in it or turn it regularly. Use a thermometer with a long probe attached, similar to a large meat thermometer, to check the temperature in your pile. When the temperature drops, give the pile a turn.

- Finished compost is dark in colour and light in texture. When you can no longer recognize what went into the compost, it is ready for use.

- Compost can be mixed into garden soil or spread on the surface as a mulch.

Images of fall: the ripening berries of the viburnum (*top left*); juicy clusters of vine-ripened grapes (*top*); tasty corn on the cob fresh from the garden (*above*). Though many people assume grapes won't grow on the prairies, numerous varieties are available for eating and wine and juice making.

OCTOBER

29

30

31

If you haven't got the time or the inclination to fuss over your compost, you can just leave it in a pile and it will eventually decompose with no added assistance from you.

Sunflowers (*below*) are synonymous with fall for many gardeners. Their bold yellow, seed-filled flower-heads celebrate the harvest season and provide treats for the birds.

It is generally a good idea to add a source of organic matter to the soil. However, if you are attempting to change the pH of the soil, it is advisable to have a soil test done prior to adding the amendments. Soil tests are done at government or private labs. These tests will tell you what the pH is, the comparative levels of sand, silt, clay and organic matter and the quantities of all required nutrients. They will also tell you what amendments to add and in what quantities to improve your soil.

There are other good amendments for soil, depending on what is required:

- Gypsum can be mixed into a clay soil along with compost to loosen the structure and allow water to penetrate.
- Elemental sulphur, peat moss or pine needles added on a regular basis can make an alkaline soil more acidic.
- Calcitic or dolomitic limestone, hydrated lime, quicklime or wood ashes can be added to an acidic soil to make it more alkaline.

Sunflowers (*above*) and other cut flowers can be found in abundance in farmers' markets throughout the province. Use them for fresh or dried table arrangements, or flower pressing for winter crafts.

NOVEMBER

*As the prairie winter settles in,
we start to forget this year's garden and turn
our thoughts to next summer.*

NOVEMBER

1

2

Faded annuals and vegetables can be pulled up and added to the compost pile.

3

4

If you have healthy willows, dogwoods, Virginia creeper or evergreens, cut a few branches to use in Christmas wreaths. Store in a cool place until needed.

5

6

7

California poppy (*left*) self-seeds, so it may pop up from year to year in the same area if left to its own devices.

D espite the inevitable frosts, a few stragglers always hang on. Flowers such as calendula, ornamental cabbage and pansies continue to bloom and provide colour, even under a light blanket of snow, until the ground starts to freeze. The ground may freeze by mid-month, but some years it doesn't until December.

THINGS TO DO

Garden tasks this month centre around finishing tucking the garden in for winter.

Harvest any remaining vegetables. Root vegetables, such as carrots, parsnips and turnips, and green vegetables, such as cabbages and broccoli, store well in a cool place, and their flavour is often improved after a touch of frost.

The garden can be quite beautiful in November, especially with a light dusting of snow on branches with persistent fruits (*right, below*).

November

8

9

Clear away tools, hoses and garden furniture before the snow flies so they won't be damaged by the cold and wet weather.

10

11

Mound mulch around the bases of semi-hardy shrubs to protect the roots and stem bases from temperature fluctuations.

12

13

The richly coloured rosettes of ornamental kale (*far right and bottom right*), which often persist into November, are reminiscent of roses (*top right*).

14

The beautiful hybrid tea rose 'Rosemary Harkness' (*left*) produces fragrant orange-yellow double blooms from summer to autumn. Like other tender hybrid teas, it should be protected from harsh prairie winter weather.

Prepare hybrid tea and other semi-hardy roses for winter early in the month. Mound dirt over the base of the rose and cover with mulch, or cover it with a cardboard box, open the top and fill around the plant with loose, quick-drying material, such as sawdust, shredded leaves or peat moss. Hold the box in place with a heavy rock on top when you are done.

Avoid completely covering perennials with mulch until the ground freezes. Mound the mulch around them, and store some extra mulch in a frost-free location to add once they are frozen. If you pile the mulch in the garden, you may find it has also frozen solid when you want to use it.

NOVEMBER

15

16

Be sure to enjoy any remaining warm days before the garden becomes the dream of next summer.

17

18

Fill your birdfeeders regularly. Well-fed birds will continue to visit your garden in summer, feeding on undesirable insects in your garden.

19

20

21

Clockwise from top right: hollyhock, hens and chicks, ice plant and lilac tolerate drought and make good choices for xeriscaping. Million bells (*left*) look great in hanging baskets, planters, beds and borders. They bloom profusely all summer and into fall surviving temperatures as low as -7°C.

If an area of your garden always seems dry, consider a xeriscape planting in that area. Many plants are drought resistant and thrive even in areas that are never watered. Yarrow, hollyhock, prickly pear cactus, black-eyed Susan, jack pine, potentilla, peashrub and cosmos are just a few of the many possibilities for a dry section of the garden.

Now that you've had the chance to observe your garden for a growing season, consider the microclimates and think about how you can put them to good use. Are any always quick to dry? Do some areas stay wet longer than others? What area is the most sheltered? Which is the least sheltered? Cater your plantings to the microclimates of your garden.

NOVEMBER

22

23

*Wait for the ground to freeze up before
protecting tender shrubs
and evergreens to ensure that all growth
has slowed for winter.*

24

25

*Spray anti-desiccantson evergreens such as
rhododendrons and cedar or provide a
protective burlap screen to prevent moisture
loss over winter.*

26

27

28

Flowers such as marsh marigolds (*left*), irises (*top
and far right*), daylilies (*centre right*) and ligularia
(*bottom right*) work well in damp areas of the garden because they prefer moist growing conditions.

BOG GARDENING

Turn a damp area into your own little bog garden. Dig out an area 35–50 cm (14–20") below ground level, line with a piece of punctured pond liner and fill with soil. The area will stay wet but still allow some water to drain away, providing a perfect location to plant moisture-loving perennials. A few to consider are

- Astilbe (*Astilbe* x *arendsii*)
- Daylily (*Hemerocallis* hybrids)
- Doronicum (*Doronicum orientale*)
- Globeflower (*Trollius europaeus*)
- Goatsbeard (*Aruncus dioicus*)
- Hosta (*Hosta* hybrids)
- Iris (*Iris ensata, Iris siberica*)
- Lady's Mantle (*Alchemilla mollis*)
- Ligularia (*Ligularia dentata* and *wilsoniana*)
- Marsh Marigold (*Caltha palustris*)
- Meadowsweet (*Filipendula rubra* and *ulmaria*)
- Primrose (*Primula japonica*)
- Rayflower (*Ligularia dentata*)

Finish collecting seeds from open-pollinated flowers and vegetables. Stored in a cool, dry place, they will be ready for planting in next year's garden.

Rodgersia (*left*) bears bold foliage and fluffy flower plumes in mid- to late summer. It does best in a site sheltered from strong winds and extreme weather. Rodgersia plants prefer moist soil and require winter protection. Plants that will need some winter protection, *clockwise from top right*: Oregon grape holly; star magnolia; gingko; azalea

The warmest, most sheltered area of your garden should be reserved for those plants that are not fully hardy here in the chilly north. Azalea, star magnolia and ginko are just a few of the many out of zone plants that have proven themselves capable of withstanding our cold winters if planted in a suitably sheltered location.

If you have a very exposed area in your garden, you can find plants that will do well there, or you can make a planting that will shelter the area. A cotoneaster hedge or group planting will break the wind and provide an attractive feature for your garden.

DECEMBER

*Amaryllis and Christmas cactus explode
into bloom and red speckled poinsettias light up
our rooms as the holidays draw near.*

DECEMBER

1

2

*If you haven't already done so,
finish mulching the garden.*

3

4

*Clean tools thoroughly and wipe them
with an oily rag to prevent them from
rusting before storing them for winter.*

5

6

7

Holly (*left*) makes an attractive addition to fresh
winter arrangements. To keep it looking its best,
keep the cut ends consistently moist.
Mugo pine and pagoda (*top right*); poplars and
spruce (*bottom right*)

Although perennials and garden beds are now buried under drifts of snow, structure, form and colour stand out in a snowy landscape. Persistent fruit, snow-covered evergreen boughs, red dogwood twigs and peeling bark draw your eye out to the garden even on the coldest days. Pleasing thoughts of spring distract us as winter shuffles in, clear blue skies and all.

THINGS TO DO

Our thoughts turn to indoor gardening though we may still have a few garden tasks to complete before we call it a year.

Gently brush snow off flexible evergreen branches. Heavy snow can weigh down upright juniper and cedar branches enough to permanently bend them downwards.

If rabbits and mice are a problem in your garden, you can protect your trees and shrubs with chicken wire. Wrap it around the plant bases and higher up the tree or shrub than you expect the snow to reach.

In December our thoughts turn to decorating for the holidays. Now is the time to use some of the flowers you dried to make potpourri, wreaths or floral arrangements.

DECEMBER

8

9

Move clay and concrete pots and statues into a dry, warm location to prevent them from cracking over winter.

10

11

Reduce watering and cease feeding houseplants.

12

13

Any herbs you are growing indoors should be kept in the brightest window you have to prevent them from becoming too straggly or dying.

14

Poinsettias (*left*) add rich colour and beauty to our homes during the dark days of December. *Clockwise from top right*: dracaena; *Cattleya* orchid; *Miltonopsis* orchid; cast iron plant

HOUSEPLANT CARE

You don't have to forget gardening completely when the snow begins to fly. All you have to do is turn your attention to indoor gardening. Houseplants clean the air, soften the hard edges of a room and provide colour, texture and interest to your home.

Just as you did for the garden outdoors, match your indoor plants to the conditions your home provides. If a room receives little light, consider houseplants that require very low light levels. Plants that like humid conditions, such as African violets, ferns and philodendrons, may do best in your bathroom where water from showering and the toilet bowl maintain higher moisture levels than in any other room. Plants that tolerate or prefer dry air, such as cacti, ficus, palms and poinsettias, will grow well with no added humidity.

15

16

Most indoor plant pests can be controlled by wiping leaves with a damp sponge. More difficult pests can be controlled with insecticidal soap.

17

18

Asparagus fern, Chinese evergreen, Kentia palm and peace lily do well in low-light areas. Cacti, jade plant, flowering maple and passion flower do well in bright light.

19

20

Although orchids are reputed to be difficult to grow, some orchids such as the moth orchid *Phalaenopsis* (*left*) are easy to grow on a windowsill. There are many thousands of species of orchids in an amazing array of sizes, shapes, colours and fragrances. Indoor water garden (*centre right*); braided lucky bamboo (*bottom right*)

21

There are three aspects of interior light to consider: intensity, duration and quality. Intensity is the difference between a south-facing window with full sun and a north-facing room with no direct sunlight. Duration is how long the light lasts in a specific location. An east-facing window will have a shorter duration of light than a south-facing window. Quality refers to the spectrum of the light. Natural light provides a broader spectrum than artificial light.

Watering is a key element to houseplant care. Over-watering can be as much of a problem as under-watering. As you did with your garden plants, water thoroughly and infrequently. Let the soil dry out a bit before watering plants. Some plants are the exception to this rule. Find out what the water requirements of your houseplants are so you will have an idea of how frequently or infrequently you will need to water.

Look for creative ways to display your plants and add humidity to your home. Indoor fountains and moisture-loving plants, such as a peace lily, in a vase of water (*top*), adds much-needed moisture to your home during the dry winter months.

22

23

*Dust on plants is more than just an eyesore.
It prevents plants from making full use
of the light they receive. Clean leaves
regularly with a damp cloth or sponge
or place them in the shower and let
the water stream wash away any dust.*

24

25

26

27

28

English ivy (*left*) that you've grown outdoors all
summer can be brought indoors and kept as a
houseplant in winter. The snake plant (*bottom right*),
is a striking, long-lived indoor plant.

Houseplants generally only need fertilizer when they are actively growing. Always use a weak fertilizer to avoid burning the roots. Never feed plants when they are very dry. Moisten the soil by watering and then feed a couple of days later.

When repotting, go up by only one size at a time. In general the new pot should be no more than 5–10 cm (2–4") larger in diameter than the previous pot. If you find your soil drying out too frequently, then you may wish to use a larger pot that will stay moist for longer.

Houseplants are more than just attractive—they clean the air in our homes. Many dangerous and common toxins, such as benzene, formaldehyde and trichloroethylene, are absorbed and eliminated by houseplants, such as spider plants (*right*).

Here are a few easy-to-grow, toxin-absorbing houseplants:

- Bamboo Palm (*Camaedorea erumpens*)
- Chinese Evergreen (*Aglaonema modestum*)
- Dragon Tree (*Dracaena marginata*)
- English Ivy (*Hedera helix*)
- Gerbera Daisy (*Gerbera jamesonii*)
- Peace Lily (*Spathiphyllum* 'Mauna Loa')
- Pot Mum (*Chrysanthemum morifolium*)
- Snake Plant (*Sansevieria trifasciata*)
- Spider Plant (*Chlorophytum cosmosum*)
- Weeping Fig (*Ficus benjamina*)

DECEMBER

29

Plants can be grouped together in large containers to more easily meet the needs of the plants. Cacti can be planted together in a gritty soil mix and placed in a dry, bright location. Moisture and humidity-loving plants can be planted in a large terrarium where moisture levels remain higher.

30

31

A bouquet of cheerful gerberas and painted daisies (*below*) will brighten a drab winter day and remind you of summer, when these flowers were growing in your garden. Cacti and rubber plants (*right*) make good houseplants because they are undemanding and tolerate the dry air found in prairie homes quite well.

Keep in mind that many common houseplants are tropical and dislike hot, dry conditions. Most houseplants will thrive in cooler, moister conditions than you will provide in your home. Always turn thermostats down at night and provide moist conditions by sitting pots on pebble trays. Water in the pebble tray can evaporate but won't soak excessively into the soil of the pot because the pebbles hold it above the water.

A bouquet of fresh flowers (*above*) is bound to brighten anyone's day, especially during winter. Spring and fall-flowering varieties from the coast and California are widely available in florist shops and grocery stores. Exotic Australian and South American flowers are the current trend, sporting vivid shades and unique forms.

RESOURCES

Books

Brickell, Christopher, T.J. Cole and J.D. Zuk, eds. 1996. *Reader's Digest A–Z Encyclopedia of Garden Plants*. The Reader's Digest Association Ltd., Montreal, PQ.

Brickell, Christopher and David Joyce. 1996. *Pruning and Training*. Dorling Kindersley, London, England.

Bubel, Nancy. 1988. *The New Seed-Starter's Handbook*. Rodale Press, Emmaus, PA.

Casselman, Bill. 1997. *Canadian Garden Words*. Little, Brown and Company (Canada) Ltd., Toronto, ON.

Courtier, Jane and Graham Clarke. 1997. *Indoor Plants: The Essential Guide to Choosing and Caring for Houseplants*. Reader's Digest, Westmount, PQ.

Ellis, B.W. and F.M. Bradley, eds. 1996. *The Organic Gardener's Handbook of Natural Insect and Disease Control*. Rodale Press, Emmaus, PA.

Flanagan, June and Donna Fremont. *The Prairie Gardener's Sourcebook*. Fifth House Publishing, Calgary, AB.

Heintzelman, Donald S. 2001. *The Complete Backyard Birdwatcher's Home Companion*. Ragged Mountain Press, Camden, ME.

Hole, Lois. 1993. *Lois Hole's Vegetable Favorites*. Lone Pine Publishing, Edmonton, AB.

— —. 1994. *Lois Hole's Bedding Plant Favorites*. Lone Pine Publishing, Edmonton, AB.

— —. 1995. *Lois Hole's Perennial Favorites*. Lone Pine Publishing, Edmonton, AB.

— —. 1996. *Lois Hole's Tomato Favorites*. Lone Pine Publishing, Edmonton, AB.

— —. 1997. *Lois Hole's Rose Favorites*. Lone Pine Publishing, Edmonton, AB.

— —. 1997. *Lois Hole's Favorite Trees and Shrubs*. Lone Pine Publishing, Edmonton, AB.

Hill, Lewis. 1991. *Secrets of Plant Propagation*. Storey Communications Inc., Pownal, VT.

Kershaw, Linda. 2003. *Manitoba Wayside Wildflowers*. Lone Pine Publishing, Edmonton, AB.

Knowles, Hugh. 1995. *Woody Ornamentals for the Prairies*. University of Alberta Press, Edmonton, AB.

Leatherbarrow, Liesbeth and Lesley Reynolds. 1999. *101 Best Plants for the Prairies,* Fifth House Publishing. Calgary, AB.

— —. 2001. *Best Bulbs for the Prairies,* Fifth House Publishing. Calgary, AB.

Mather, Jan. 1997. *The Prairie Rose Garden*. Red Deer College Press, Red Deer, AB.

McHoy, Peter. 2002. *Houseplants*. Hermes House, New York, NY.

McVicar, Jekka. 1997. *Jekka's Complete Herb Book*. Raincoast Books, Vancouver, BC.

Merilees, Bill. 1989. *Attracting Backyard Wildlife: A Guide for Nature Lovers*. Voyageur Press, Stillwater, MN.

Robinson, Peter. 1997. *Complete Guide to Water Gardening*. Reader's Digest, Westmount, PQ.

Scalise, Karyn. 1996. *Wildlife Gardening in Saskatchewan: Building Backyard Biodiversity*. Printwest, Regina, SK.

Thompson, Peter. 1992. *Creative Propagation: A Grower's Guide*. Timber Press, Portland, OR.

Toop, Edgar W. 1993. *Annuals for the Prairies*. Lone Pine Publishing, Edmonton, AB.

Toop, Edgar W. and Sara Williams. 1991. *Perennials for the Prairies*. University of Alberta Extension Press, Edmonton, AB.

Warke, Terry and Paul Harris. 1998. *The Prairie Water Garden*. Red Deer College Press, Red Deer, AB.

Williams, Sara. 1997. *Creating the Prairie Xeriscape: Water Efficient, Low Maintenance Gardening*. University Extension Press, University of Saskatchewan, Saskatoon, SK.

Online Resources

Attracting Wildlife. How to make your backyard inviting to wildlife.
www.attracting-wildlife-to-your-garden.com

Bedrock Seed Bank. Provides seed from over 630 varieties to enable gardeners to re-establish native varieties.
www.albertadirectory.net/bedrockseed/

Canadian Gardening. Ask the expert section and list of gardening catalogues.
www.canadiangardening.com/home.html

Canadian Organic Growers. Fantastic information on organic growing.
www.cog.ca

Canadian Wildlife Federation Wild About Gardening. Safe and environmentally friendly ways to attract wildlife.
http://www.wildaboutgardening.org/

Colleen's Corner, Welcome to the Garden Path. A Manitoba gardener shares experiences and advice.
www.colleenscorner.com

Composting Council of Canada. A national nonprofit organization that promotes composting.
www.compost.org

Evergreen Foundation. Provides tools to create healthy outdoor spaces.
www.evergreen.ca/en/index.html

I Can Garden. Information and a forum where you can contact gardeners from across Canada and beyond.
www.icangarden.com/

Manitoba Gardening. A gardening site with a variety of topics of interest to Manitoba gardeners.
www.manitobagardening.com

Northern Gardening Forum. List of gardening forums intended for northern USA but used by many Canadians.
http://forums.gardenweb.com/forums/north/

Organic Gardening—Canada. Information and resources.
www.coab.ca/gardening.htm

Prairie Frontier. Create an easy-to-maintain landscape inviting to wildlife, butterflies and birds.
www.prairiefrontier.com/pages/families/attracts.html

Seeds of Diversity Canada. Gardeners who save and share seeds of rare, unusual and heritage plants.
www.seeds.ca/en.htm

Turf Resource Center and The Lawn Institute. The latest data on turfgrass.
www.TurfGrassSod.org
www.LawnInstitute.com

University of Manitoba, School of Agriculture. List of gardening courses.
www.umanitoba.ca/faculties/afs/school/gardening.html

Soil-Testing Facilities

Manitoba Provincial Soil Testing Lab
Dept. of Soil Sciences
Room 262, Ellis Building
University of Manitoba
Winnipeg, MB R3T 2N2
1-204-474-9257

Norwest Labs
Agricultural Services Complex
203-545 University Crescent
Winnipeg, MB R3T 5S6
1-204-982-8630 or 1-800-483-3448
www.norwestlabs.com

Horticultural Societies

Charleswood Horticultural Society
777 Berkley Street
Winnipeg, MB R3K 1K2
1-204-895-2574

East Kildonan Garden Club
1-204-661-0836
email: awheeler@awnet.com
www.icangarden.com/clubs/EKGC/

The Friends of the Assiniboine Park Conservatory
15 Conservatory Drive
Winnipeg, MB R3P 2N5
1-204-837-4324 or 1-204-986-5537
email: kchipman@mb.sympatico.ca

Manitoba Horticultural Association
2 Westmount Bay
Winnipeg, MB R2J 1Y8
1-204-256-2745
fax: 1-204-257-4546
email: m.h.a@shaw.ca

Manitoba People and Plants
Box 302, Killarney, MB R0K 1G0
1-204-523-8570
email: nancy@perennialbliss.com
www.perennialbliss.com

The Manitoba Regional Lily Society
http://www.manitobalilies.ca/

St. James Horticultural Society
1-204-837-6854
email: avferris@shaw.ca
Transcona Garden Club
8 Virden Crescent
Winnipeg, MB R2C 2A4
1-204-222-0236

West Kildonan Horticultural Society
1-204-694-8147
email: annyou@autobahn.mb.ca

Gardens to Visit

Agriculture and Agri-Food Canada
Brandon Research Centre Grounds
18th Street & Grand Valley Road
Brandon, MB
1-204-726-7650
email: rmarch@em.agr.ca

Agriculture and Agri-Food Canada
Morden Research Station Arboretum and Grounds
E of Morden, junction of Hwy 3 and
Provincial Road 100
Unit 100–101, Route 100
Morden, MB R6M 1Y5
1-204-822-4471 or 1-204-822-7201
http://res2.agr.ca/winnipeg/m1_e.htm

Altona, MB
Sunflower Capital of Canada
Visit mid- to late summer to view abundant
fields of sunflowers
1-204-324-6468
email: info@townofaltona.com
www.townofaltona.com/community/
attractions

Assiniboine Park
2355 Corydon Avenue
Winnipeg, MB R3P 0R5
1-204-986-6531 (Leo Mol Sculpture
Garden)
1-204-986-5537 (Conservatory)
http://www.winterpeg.com/Town/
Assiniboine-Park.htm
http://www.city.winnipeg.mb.ca/cms/parks/
envserv/conserv/default.htm

Captain Kennedy Museum and Tea Room
12 km N of Winnipeg on Hwy 9
Lot 63, River Road
St. Andrews, MB
1-204-334-2498
www.rmofstandrews.com/index2.html

Elizabeth Park
N end of Elizabeth Street & Mountain Avenue
Neepawa, MB
1-204-476-8811 or 1-877-633-7292
email: npwchamb@escape.cc
www.town.neepawa.mb.ca/lily

English Gardens at Riding Mountain National Park
Between Minnedosa and Dauphin on Hwy 10
Riding Mountain Park Plus People
Box 9, Wasagaming, MB R0J 2H0

1-204-848-7284 or 1-800-707-8480
email: RMNP_info@PCH.gc.ca
www.parkscanada.gc.ca/riding

Frank Skinner Arboretum Trail
1 km E off Hwy 83, 23 km S of Roblin
Frank Skinner Arboretum Corp.
Box 1221, Roblin, MB R0L 1P0
1-204-564-2336 or 1-204-564-2317
email: skinnerh@mb.sympatico.ca
www.roblinmanitoba.com/business/
arbor/skinner.htm

Gertrude Williams Memorial Park
Main Street (Hwy 16) and 3rd Street
Neepawa, MB
1-204-476-8811 or 1-877-633-7292
email: npwchamb@escape.cc
www.town.neepawa.mb.ca/lily

International Peace Garden
Turtle Mountain Provincial Park
20 km S of Boissevain on Hwy 10
(at Manitoba/North Dakota border)
PO Box 419, Boissevain, MB R0K 0E0
1-204-534-2510
www.peacegarden.com

Island Park Arboretum
Parks Division
97 Saskatchewan Avenue E
Portage la Prairie, MB R1N 0L8
1-204-239-8346
www.city.portage-la-prairie.mb.ca/
community/tourism.html

Kildonan Park
2021 Main Street
Winnipeg, MB
1-204-986-7623
http://www.tourism.winnipeg.mb.ca/tw
Leisure/tourismWinnipeg_thingsToSee_
A15.html

King's Park
King's Drive at Kilkenny Drive
Winnipeg, MB
http://www.arch.umanitoba.ca/greenmap/
pages/GrnMp_Kingspk/

Living Prairie Museum
2795 Ness Avenue
Winnipeg, MB R3J 3S4
1-204-832-0167
email: prairie@mbnet.mb.ca
http://www.city.winnipeg.mb.ca/cms/parks/
envserv/interp/living.htm

Memorial Provincial Heritage Park
(across from the Manitoba Legislature)
Memorial Drive
Winnipeg, MB
1-800-214-6497 or
(Winnipeg only)1-204- 945-6784
www.gov.mb.ca/natres/parks/heritage_
parks/memorial_main.html

CKNOWLEDGEMENTS

We would especially like to thank our fellow garden writers Don Williamson and Alison Beck for their many contributions and discussions. As well, we thank all those who contributed suggestions and advice on both content and style during the creation of this book.

We are grateful to photographers Tamara Eder, Tim Matheson and Robert Ritchie, Marilyn MacAra, Dean Didur and to the many people who opened their gardens for us to photograph.

We would also like to thank Shane Kennedy, Nancy Foulds, editor Sandra Bit and book designer and Master Gardener Heather Markham. Thanks also to Gerry Dotto for the cover design and to Ian Sheldon for the lovely corner flourishes that grace the pages. Others helped in various ways, close-cropping photos and providing stylistic solutions, and we thank them all.

Cover page photos:
January—spruce bough
February—frosty elm leaves
March—persistent fruit on crabapple tree
April—primroses and tulips
May—apple blossoms
June—hosta
July—shrub rose "The Fairy"
August—dahlias
September—viburnum
October—pumpkins
November—hoarfrost at sunset
December—poinsettias